WHAT ANGLICANS BELIEVE

What Anglicans Believe

DAVID L. EDWARDS

Dean of Norwich

MOWBRAY
LONDON & OXFORD

© David L. Edwards 1974
Text set in Intertype Baskerville
and printed and bound in Great Britain by
Richard Clay (The Chaucer Press) Ltd, Bungay, Suffolk

ISBN 0 264 66145 1

First published 1974 by
A. R. Mowbray & Co. Ltd.
Saint Thomas House,
Becket Street, Oxford, OX1 1SJ
Reprinted 1975
Reprinted 1977
Reprinted 1980

Contents

Preface

I was asked to write a short book which would sum up what members of the Church of England and other Anglicans believe nowadays. At first I refused, because I could not help knowing what problems would be involved. Some Anglicans believe one thing, some another. Some are more Catholic, others more Evangelical; some are traditional, others are in revolt against tradition. Who am I to decide which group is right at which point? And that is not the only problem. Some potential readers will complain that a book is too simple, others that it is not simple enough; some that it asks too many questions, others that it gives too many answers. So I said no. Then, months later, I changed my mind and said yes, because I grew convinced that a book was needed, despite all the inevitable problems and all the likely criticisms. If I can help a single person to see what one Anglican (myself) believes about the things that matter, the book will be worthwhile. In particular I have daughters and a son who are not yet confirmed as full members of the Church of England, and I offer them this book with love.

Writing this book has proved as difficult as I expected, but I was fortunate enough to receive the detailed criticisms of Donald Allchin, Michael Jacob, William Purcell, John Stockdale and Margaret Webster. I only hope that not too many of the difficulties show in the book itself, which is meant to be both informal and enjoyable.

I use again some sentences from my book on *This*

Church of England (1962), by kind permission of the holders of the copyright, the Central Board of Finance of the Church of England.

I am also grateful to the Oxford and Cambridge University Presses for permission to quote from the *New English Bible*, 2nd Edition Copyright 1970, and to SPCK on behalf of the Registrars of the Provinces of Canterbury and York for permission to quote from *Alternative Series Series 3, An Order for Holy Communion*.

D.L.E.

I

We believe in God

Is IT reasonable to believe in God? Nowadays many people think it isn't, although not many people say that they are convinced atheists. ('Atheism' means that you are sure there is no God. 'Agnosticism' means that you can't decide whether there is or isn't. Many people are agnostics.)

We must face the fact that belief in God can easily turn into mere superstition or sentimentality, which is against all reason. People can have gods whose job is to give them assistance in their private ambitions – or to help their tribe or nation to win a war or to grow a good harvest. That is a dangerous kind of nonsense. Or people can have a god who is like a doll in the cupboard or like an old man with a beard in the sky – nice enough, but unable to do anything that matters.

It is also a fact that people can say that evil attitudes are commanded by the god they worship. They can say that their god wishes them to be arrogant, intolerant and cruel – or that their god wishes them to contradict what is known scientifically. People calling themselves Christians have tried to justify their evil attitudes in these ways.

It is, however, possible to seek the real God. Indeed, it is not only possible – nowadays it is *necessary* if you are to believe in God.

In the old days almost everyone had to accept the beliefs which were taken for granted in the society around them, and one of the beliefs it was dangerous to question was belief in God (or gods). But in our society there is religious freedom, which from every point of view is a great gain. It frees those who don't believe from the need to pretend. And it brings many benefits to sincerely religious people. For it means that you have to make your own search to find God – just as you have to make your own search to find a wife or a husband. In that adventure, you will grow spiritually. You have to make up your own mind – and so your mind is made your own.

No words, however pure or sacred, will fully describe God. Indian spiritual teachers say something about God to which we ought to listen. They say: 'Not that! Not that!' The same emphasis on the mystery of God is found in the Bible. For God can never be pinned down like a dead butterfly, reduced to a formula or reproduced in a photograph. No talk about God can be completely accurate, because all such talk must use words which were invented to describe the world or man – not God. Like shots which always miss their target, human words will always fall short of the glory of God. But the words can show in what direction the glory lies; however imperfectly, they can point to the reality. For example, when we say that God is 'personal' we must remember that he cannot be a person as we are people. He must be much more. But the word 'personal' points to the reality that, if he is real, God cannot be *less* than personal – for he cannot be less than us.

God has been well described as 'the most real thing there is'. The trouble is that we often keep the idea of God in a separate compartment of our mind – and we often keep all the things that are immediately important to us (health, money, sex, music, our job, our family, today's news, a personal tragedy) in other compartments which we think of as more realistic. But if God is real, then he is *more* real than the greatest thing or the best thing or the worst thing in the rest of our experience.

There is no *proof* that God is real – if by 'proof' we

mean the way it can be proved that this book exists or that 2+2=4. God (if real) is just too big to be fitted into that kind of proof. And even if you make up your mind that God is real, you will never 'know' this in the way that you can know the truth of a formula in chemistry or a fact in the newspaper. Until you die you will always need faith and your faith will always be attacked by doubts, since if you 'believe' you always have to admit that you may be wrong, even if you only admit it to yourself. If you believe, it is like swimming in water – where you could equally well drown. This may alarm you. But just as there can be no sure proof of God, so also there can be no sure *disproof*. You simply have to decide for yourself – and that goes for atheists too. After a shipwreck, some decide to swim. And others decide to drown!

There is a kind of proof which you can have when thinking about God – and a kind of knowledge, too. It is the knowledge that you have when you say you 'believe' in a friend. It is the proof that you have when you love someone else and find yourself loved back. That love is proved to you deep down, although someone looking on can say: 'They don't really love each other – I see no proof.' And deep down you *know* the person you love, although someone looking on can say, 'I can't see what he sees in her.' Your relationship with God can become like that. You still will not have complete certainty, but you will have enough confidence to decide that for all practical purposes you are prepared to bet your life that God is there.

Of course you run the risk of being wrong. But just as a scientist makes an experiment in order to test a theory, so you can put belief in God to the test – by living in the light of it. Then you will find yourself increasingly assured about God's reality.

Sometimes this kind of assurance can come to you suddenly, like a flash. Some people have dramatic experiences which persuade them that God is real. Even in those cases, however, the search for the real God has probably been going on for a long time. Normally it takes a long time to reach the strong relationship with God that produces confidence.

Don't believe the people who promise you that you can have the vision by swallowing a drug. What people see when under the influence of a drug is an illusion produced by chemistry, and it quickly fades – leaving behind problems which can be very serious. And don't believe the people who tell you that you can't find God without reading strange books or going to distant countries. God is closer to you than your feet or your hands or your breath, and he has been found by many millions in your own country's way as well as in the ways of other nations.

The best way, in England or in India or wherever you are, is to be quiet before this mystery – to meditate, that means thinking calmly, slowly, deeply. Think about God much more than about yourself, want him more than you want anything for yourself, but try to make sure that there is love in your heart and peace in your mind, so that you are not distracted by any foolishness. Say to God: 'If you are real, give me the eyes to glimpse your reality.' Ask God to show himself to you as he really is, even if it means showing you that you will have to change your own ways of thinking and behaving.

You will find that you have to concentrate, and that you have to do so again and again. It is a discipline, like learning a language or learning to ride a bicycle. But many of the finest characters and greatest minds in history have made the same search before you. And people who seriously seek the real God find that no one goes unrewarded. So you have to say to yourself: 'This search is the most important task I shall ever attempt. This adventure is going to take all I have, but my aim is to find the greatest treasure that could possibly exist.'

When you seek the meaning in life, you are seeking God. For there cannot be much meaning if there is no

God! And when you seek God, you express a hunger. Every other hunger corresponds with some food which can satisfy it. Despite your doubts and hesitations about belief in God, the alternative seems to you grim – a largely meaningless life, a largely frustrated hunger of the spirit for meaning. Doesn't that mean that deep down you are already inclining towards the decision to believe in God? A French mathematician, Blaise Pascal, wrote three hundred years ago that he seemed to hear God saying to him: 'Comfort yourself, you would not seek me if you had not found me.' And a great saint, Augustine of Hippo, looked back over his long search for God with this prayer: 'You have made us for yourself, and our heart is unquiet until it rests in you.'

Remind yourself of the marvellous and often alarming features which have persuaded many to worship the mighty God – a glorious sunset over a city, countless stars in the night sky, the ocean in a storm, mountains, lions, the music of a symphony. (What is missing from that list?) Meditate also on the small things: an obscure animal so perfectly adapted to life, a rose, bird-song, light on water, dew on grass, a human baby, a girl's face, an athlete's health. (What is missing?) These things may be clues to aid your own search for the answer to the riddle of existence.

There are many things about your life, about man's life on the earth, and about the universe, that make it hard to believe in God. Face up to them – otherwise you will be told that your faith isn't honest, and you may agree with your critics. There is darkness around us. But also light! For many things about your life, about man's life on the earth, and about the universe, are indeed hard to explain if there is no God and therefore no good purpose running through it all. Atheism has its problems. . . .

Why does anything exist, rather than nothing?

If the universe is nothing more than an accident, how has it happened that it contains so much order and so much beauty? It has been said that it works like a machine, yet sleeps like a picture.

The machinery of evolution can be understood. There are many mutations (genetic changes), and out of these the fittest – those best adapted to the struggle for life – survive. So chance comes into it. But does the whole process consist of nothing more than chances which are selected by the iron necessities of life? Is the universe merely a lottery or a Bingo hall? If so, how has it happened that there has been such amazing progress? How has sheer chance produced Shakespeare and Beethoven, Einstein and Rembrandt?

If man can understand *nothing* about any purpose in the universe, how has it happened that he can understand so much else? Looking up a telescope or down a microscope, the scientist increasingly understands what he sees. The poet, the artist or the musician is able to celebrate the order and the beauty. How has the mind of man happened?

If in the end human life has no meaning in the universe, how has it happened that the universe has produced this home for man? If the universe mocks the love and the courage in man, why does man have this character? It was said long ago, in Ancient Greece, that man believes in beauty, truth and goodness. Everyone has at least glimmerings of those beliefs. Many people regard them as more important than comfort, ease or ambition. People often struggle to create beauty, to reach the truth, to do what seems right – whatever the cost. People are happy to spend their lives in these tasks, and they are prepared to die for the sake of these causes. Man can never rid himself of these basic beliefs in beauty, truth and goodness – and he does not usually want to. How has it happened that such a freak has been born?

These are questions which atheists find it hard to answer – as believers in God find it hard to answer the problem of the existence of evil. In the end you have to decide whether the good seems to you more significant than the evil. You have to make up your own mind whether you are to be guided by the light you see, or by the darkness. People can meet this challenge in different ways which are equally honest. But there is no need to agree with the atheists that every thought about God has been proved to be a complete illusion. On the contrary, much of the evidence points to God – the God who is there beyond the ideas and pictures about him.

These thoughts can help you to believe, as a map made by previous travellers can guide you on a long journey into a strange country. But no argument can *force* you to believe. Only your own experience, as you understand it, can give you a living faith in the real God. So this question about God comes addressed to you personally.

2

The Father

WHEN YOU stand at a cross-roads, one fact is certain. You won't get where you want to be if you sit down! In much the same way, if you don't feel that the road to God is signposted clearly enough for you to travel along it, sooner or later you will give up asking and trying. Although you may call yourself an agnostic, for all practical purposes you will be an athesist.

But you will go forward along a road if you trust the sign. And in much the same way, if you decide to trust the signs pointing to the reality of God, you will find that as you make the journey of faith your faith grows both stronger and also more realistic.

You will acknowledge God as Creator. But be careful! That does not mean having a theory about how the universe began or how man began. Scientists are the only people competent to discuss such questions – and even scientists do not yet have all the answers. Believing in God the Creator means one answer to the questions *why* the universe began and *why* man so surprisingly emerged. It also means one answer to the questions *why* the universe continues and *why* man survives.

The answer is that God wished the universe and man into existence *out of love* – and God has not changed his mind. God loves things and people, and that love is what gives them their life. Believing in God the Creator means thanking God for this gift of life, and it also means realising more and more that everything and everyone still depend utterly on this gift which is more wonderful than words can describe. The universe minus God would equal nothing. No one could survive for a second without the Creator.

If you decide that God is real, you will acknowledge him as Ruler. But be careful! We should not pretend that everything that happens is just what God wants. The truth is that many events are beyond our understanding – and, in so far as we do understand them, many events seem contrary to God's purpose. We live in a world of mysteries and tragedies. If God is the source of all that exists, he must allow these events to happen – why, we cannot tell fully. God is not a dictator, but believing in God as Ruler means trusting that God's good purpose will in the end conquer. Even when we are surrounded by evil and almost overwhelmed by it, we can trust – because of what we have glimpsed of God's power and reliability.

We can understand why so many people have believed in more than one god. One part of life seems so different from another that it is tempting to say that each part has its own ruler. So one god sends sunshine, and another god sends rain; one god looks after one country, and another god looks after its neighbour; one god is real on Sunday, and another on Monday. But always progress in religion comes from people saying: however difficult it is to be sure of this unity, the universe is one, life is one, life's meaning is one, God the Creator and Ruler is one.

If you believe in God but keep an honest awareness of the evil which is also real, you will be in no danger of using the word 'God' and meaning by it only nature. You will find yourself thinking along different lines. God is better than nature. He opposes much that exists, for he is 'holy' – a word which means specially, uniquely, divinely good. God can do this because he is (so to speak) *beyond* all that exists although also *within* it. God is in everything, but he is more. All space is (so to speak) his body, but he is also beyond space, 'infinite'. And all time is (so to

17

speak) his life, but he is also beyond time, 'eternal'. What a craftsman makes (for example, a chair or a film) is his – but there is more to him than that; and what God creates and rules does not exhaust his endless life.

These are difficult thoughts and if we go too far into them we soon find ourselves out of our depth, trying to talk about matters far beyond our understanding and ending up by talking nonsense. But *some* of these difficult ideas ought to be familiar to every thoughtful believer, since they do arise out of the experience of the journey of faith.

Fortunately for us, Jesus put his own teaching about God in a simple way. There are two key ideas in it.

The first is that God is taking action which will show the power of his love. He will show that he *is* Creator, and Ruler, and good. In other words, *the 'kingdom' (which means 'rule') of God is coming*. Jesus taught that nothing matters more than being alert and ready to respond to this action by God. This is an extremely practical matter. As you live each day, your biggest job is to serve the 'kingdom' of God. As you watch TV or read the newspaper or meet your neighbours or go to work, you have to be quick to spot the ways in which God's purpose is being obeyed or resisted in the world today. This gives a wealth of meaning to your life and to the world's.

When you read the gospels in the Bible carefully, you will find that Jesus's favourite method of teaching was to tell a story (a parable). Almost always each story has one big point, and almost always that point is to make people more alert and ready as the kingdom of God comes. All the material in these stories was taken from the daily life familiar to Jesus and his first hearers. It is exciting and valuable if you work out for yourself some stories drawn from the life around you, to make the same point.

The second key idea is that, even before his kingdom has fully come, *God can be prayed to as 'Father'*. The Lord's Prayer, which is a simple pattern for all Christian prayer, begins 'Father!' In his letter Paul twice quoted the actual word originally used by Jesus. It is *Abba*. The equivalent is our 'Dad' or 'Daddy'. Does that seem childish? Actually Jesus was the opposite of childish. He used this word to teach a very mature understanding of God.

To call God 'Father!' is only a way of speaking, and if you prefer it you are free to think of God as 'mother' or as 'friend'. What matters is that this use of human figures *is* a way of speaking – to God. Instead of keeping silence at a distance, we speak up and come closer to God, although we know that God is greater than we can imagine. The Lord's Prayer reminds us of this when it immediately adds that the Father to whom we pray is beyond space and time, or 'heavenly'. And the meaning is not at all sentimental. The Lord's Prayer teaches this, too – when it says that God's 'name' or nature is 'holy'. To remember this is to worship. It is said about a man who is very much in love with a woman: 'you can see he worships her'. People may have an attitude close to worship towards a star in entertainment or sport – or towards a new bicycle or car. All the fascination, delight and respect felt here are no more than clues to what a worshipper of God feels.

So this description of God as 'Father!' needs to be qualified by the thought-provoking words, 'heavenly' and 'holy'. But to Jesus, the other ideas about God were all less satisfactory than 'Father!' This word expressed not only his attitude to God as a boy but also his reliance on God as a man – a reliance tested by much disappointment and suffering. Jesus was a poor man; a lonely, misunderstood man; a man who expected a terribly cruel death.

We can find here clues to the mystery why God permits so much evil in his world. A good father may be very loving and yet *not* want his children to lead a soft life – because the strength which is developed by coping with tough problems cannot be got in any other way. And a good father will not force what he thinks good on his children. He leaves it to them to make up their own minds, preferring that they should choose the good freely. It is clear that God gives us a life full of problems and allows us much freedom, however dangerous this may be. And the explanation is this: he is 'Father!'

That can change your whole outloook. For here is a view of the world which treats it as a home. The world is no longer a jumble you can't make sense of. It is no longer hostile and frightening (as some pagans think it is, believing that it is under the control of hostile gods, devils and ghosts). However vast or dark it may seem, the place where we live is a house under a father. So wherever we go, we can feel at home – or at least we can try!

If we have that view of the world, we treat it as a home. That means being happy in it – and honouring it. The other people in it belong to our family, whatever the colour of their skins or the sound of their talk. In their veins is the same red blood that runs in ours, and in their hearts are the same mixed feelings. And the whole earth deserves our respect, just as we respect (instead of damaging) the walls and the furniture of our home. The soil, water and air of this planet are precious. The earth's beauty, efficiency and (often!) comfort are marvellous. But this is not the way we always treat the world in practice. If this were our daily attitude, there would not be so much bitter conflict and misery in the news, and the future of man on the earth would not be in doubt. We have failed, and we know it. So we feel about our lives as a whole as we feel about some disgraceful thing we have done. *We feel guilty.*

Many people nowadays feel dissatisfied with their lives, but they don't think they ought to feel guilty, because they don't feel responsible. They blame it on their parents, or their governments, or their glands. They say that they can't help it, for they are entirely the creatures of circumstances. To such people, the message of Jesus that they are like guilty children saying 'sorry' to a father is *good* news – because it is the message that they are more than the stooges of fate and more than pathological cases. The real fault is in themselves! They could have helped it! Whatever handicaps they may have inherited, however damaging their environment may be, they are, when all is said and done, personally responsible for what they are. Despite all their circumstances, their wills are to some extent free. That is a great claim to make about the dignity of man, and you have to think about your own experience to find out whether or not it is true. At least you will agree that it is not a weak thing, to feel guilty before God your Father.

It is useless – indeed, dangerous – to wallow in feelings of guilt. When we have such feelings, we long for an opportunity to own up and clear the air – to express our guilt and get rid of it. Jesus announced that such an opportunity exists. It is possible to go to God as we would go to an understanding and affectionate father. We can say 'sorry' to the Creator and the Ruler – and we can be heard. In the great traditional words, we can 'confess' our 'sin'. And whenever anyone turns to God in that way, God wipes away the past – whatever the past may have been. God does not do this grudgingly. God loves doing it, for he does it out of love. So to speak, God gives a party. Jesus often said that his message was like an invitation to a party.

Instead of guilt, there is *gratitude* in the hearts of those who respond. Almost everyone enjoys life on the whole, and often feels thankful for it. But atheists have no one to thank – just as they have no one to whom they can say 'sorry'. A person who worships God as Father will want to fill his or her prayers with thanksgiving for all the good things of life, which are without exception now valued as gifts coming from God. When we receive gifts, for example at Christmas, we feel that the fun is spoiled if the label gets lost because then we 'don't know who it's from'. Half the pleasure of getting a gift is knowing whom to thank.

A Christian has a deep sense of happy gratitude to God. The Christian attitude is sometimes thought to be a fatuously hearty optimism. It is not. Christianity is sensitive to suffering, it is realistic about the power of evil, and it knows sadness. But what can sadden those who serve the everlasting joy? The Christian life is sometimes said to be a matter of keeping rules. It is not. There is discipline here. But like sons and daughters who love their parents, the Christian shows by practical behaviour how much he or she enjoys what the Father is – and what the Father gives. Christian prayer is sometimes said to be chiefly asking for things. It is not. There is honest conversation there about what we need. But the Christian in his prayer is full of thankfulness because the Christian knows how many reasons he has for being thankful.

The life of a happy family provides one more clue to the meaning of Christianity, and it is the most important clue of all. Unless the family has been tragically broken up by bitterness, every son or daughter knows that nothing can change the basic attitude of parents. Whatever the son or the daughter does, the father carries on being a father and the mother remains a mother. And if you believe in God the Father, you believe that you are *loved* – not only the 'good' bits of you but *you*, as you really are now. You belong. You are accepted. You have your place in the family, and nothing can take it away. This doesn't mean that you become lazily content with what you are. It does mean that you accept what you are – as the place to begin becoming what you think God wants you to be. You no longer hate or underestimate yourself. For if your Father who made you loves you, who are you to disagree?

3

We believe in Jesus Christ

IT SOUNDS like John Williams, or Jane Smith, this name 'Jesus Christ'. But the word 'Christ' is not a surname like Williams or Smith. It comes from a Greek word translating the Hebrew word 'Messiah', which here means king. It is a word full of meaning historically – as is shown by (for example) Handel's masterpiece in music, *Messiah*. So the phrase 'Jesus the Christ' immediately shows us that this first-century Jew, Joshua of Nazareth, has been regarded as a great leader among men – as the King of the Jews. But the fact that few people today normally think about a 'Messiah' is a reminder that if Jesus is to be described in the twentieth century it must be in words which have a modern meaning.

This is worth thinking about carefully. For Jesus has had a greater influence than any other man in the whole course of history. Almost everyone would agree that it has been an influence for great good. Indeed, very many millions of people (not all of them Christians) would call him the best man who has ever lived. But Christians want to say more: that in the life of Jesus, *God is disclosed*.

Nothing less than that! There was darkness surrounding man's search for God – now a light has shone. When man cried to God, God often seemed silent – now a voice has spoken. That is what Christians believe about Jesus, and it is worth taking trouble to work out the meaning of these beliefs in a way that is real for us.

We can begin with solid history, for it is certain that

Jesus lived in Palestine a little more than nineteen hundred years ago. It is also certain that he was executed by the Roman punishment of crucifixion, which shows that the Romans then occupying Palestine thought that he was guilty of being a rebel or of encouraging rebellion. No description of Jesus by the Romans survives, although the historians Tacitus and Suetonius mention him. The evidence that exists makes it certain, however, that Jesus was not a rebel in the ordinary sense of that word. This evidence consists almost entirely of some of the letters written by Paul within about thirty years of the death of Jesus – and four gospels which are not full biographies but which do contain much reliable information. Coming from five very different sources, this evidence enables us to reconstruct a kind of portrait of the character of Jesus. And it shows us a man whose rebellion was religious, not political.

His message was revolutionary because he announced that God's 'kingdom' was about to come – indeed, that it had already begun to come. Jesus was a Jew. His mind had been formed by the Jewish religion. But while the rest of the Jews waited for a Messiah who would be a national military leader, Jesus claimed that God was already acting decisively to show his rule and love – not by defeating the Jews' enemies in a war but by answering doubters, healing the sick, and assuring sinners of forgiveness. In particular, Jesus claimed that God could now be known as Father.

This teaching was brilliantly expressed in short stories or powerful sayings. Much of it was remembered, and some of it was written down in four gospels (probably between thirty and sixty years after Jesus's crucifixion). But the evidence suggests that it was not the teaching that made the main impact. In fact, the gospels state that a great deal of the teaching was not understood at the time by even the closest followers of Jesus. What made the impact was that Jesus lived as he taught. He not only said that God was answering doubters – he commanded some people to leave everything and follow him. He not only said that God was healing the sick – he cured some people, even when it meant breaking the religious law that no work was to be done on the 'Sabbath' (Saturday). He not only said that God was forgiving sinners – he had friendly meals with some people who were notorious. He not only said that God was doing something new – for some people, he made a new start possible. His own life was new – and so was theirs.

And this life went on *after his crucifixion* – not only in the influence which heroes often have, and not only in the memory of his character, but much more personally and powerfully. He was tortured to death in public (a hateful memory for his friends to have), yet his followers claimed that they felt his presence as surely as in the days when he had walked and talked with them along the roads of Galilee, as surely as on the evenings when, gathering his friends like a family, he had divided the loaf and poured out the wine. Their mysterious meetings with Jesus after his death were experiences which transformed their lives – giving them a new confidence, a new happiness and a new conviction that they were united with their Master and could never be separated from him. Their minds had been confused and their hearts broken; but now they were full of courage and faith, ready for hard lives and hard deaths. *Something happened* to change these men and women. That 'something' we call the 'resurrection' of Jesus.

Was the resurrection an experience in the mind? Clearly it was – but it was not dreamed up by these people. They responded to an event which happened and which convinced them. Was the resurrection of Jesus physical? The evidence says that the tomb of Jesus was empty, and that his 'risen' body could be seen and touched. This is evidence which will be taken very seriously by modern people who have been impressed by

Jesus himself – and by the moral and spiritual power of the first Christians. Although it is very strange evidence, many people would agree that very strange things happen in this world (especially in those events said to be communications with the dead which are investigated by 'psychical research'). But the four gospels describe the 'risen' body of Jesus as no ordinary body – it could go through doors, appear and disappear. It is impossible to know exactly what happened. But all Christians have good grounds for believing that something extraordinary, something of the very greatest significance, did happen.

After it, the whole world was seen in a new light. The men and women who were prepared to follow Jesus could know in their hearts that he could never be defeated. That was their light. And the same light has come to Christians ever since. To live as people who believe in the resurrection of Jesus is to live triumphantly, with a happiness which can never be taken away.

And ever since the resurrection happened, Christians have known that Jesus's own good news about the 'kingdom' and the Fatherhood of God is no longer enough. The Christian message certainly repeats what Jesus taught. But it is also now a message about Jesus himself. The followers of Jesus were soon nicknamed *Christianoi* or 'Christ-people' because they were always talking about Jesus Christ. To them, the supreme fact was that they had a personal relationship with the living Christ.

The two greatest thinkers in that first Christian generation, St Paul and St John, put their most magnificent eloquence into the task of stating what Jesus Christ meant in his own person as well as in his teaching. Inevitably they stated this mostly by describing Jesus as the climax of the Old Testament. In the course of a long debate among those great men whom we call the 'Fathers of the Church' the description of Jesus Christ which is called 'orthodox' emerged, to be accepted in seven great Councils of the Church between the years 325 and 787. This description of Jesus Christ was based on St Paul and St John but expressed in terms of a Greek philosophy which is no longer current. What matters most in it can be put very simply in the language of today.

Not only was the teaching of Jesus inspired by God. The whole life of Jesus was itself, from its beginning, an action by God – *the* action to reach and save us. The life of Jesus was the expression of God's own life in a human life. God, who is beyond space and time, has expressed himself in all that exists – but supremely he has embodied his life in a man who was born and died.

As John put it in his first chapter, the creation of the universe was like God uttering a mighty word – and in the life of Jesus Christ that Word actually 'became flesh'! For the life of God was enfleshed (which is what the Latin word behind our 'incarnate' means) – made a baby's flesh, made the flesh of a man who was hungry, weary, lonely and sorrowful, made coloured flesh, made poor flesh, made the flesh of a man who died in agony. Jesus was fully human, but the humanity of Jesus was used by God to show his love, and for this great purpose it was the perfect instrument. In the man Jesus of Nazareth, the love of God walked the earth and was nailed to wood.

That is what the life of Jesus Christ was. *And is!* For that life has never ended. Certainly he lived and died in Palestine, but if you stop his biography there you cannot make sense of the experiences of countless Christians since his death. Jesus is alive today. He is your contemporary. He is near you, whatever your situation may be. You cannot see him – but that will not stop you knowing the difference which he makes to your life, in many practical ways, if you are willing to walk with him through the problems. Listen to what one of the first Christians experienced about Jesus (in the Revelation of

John, 1.18): 'Do not be afraid. I am the first and the last, and I am the living one; for I was dead and now I am alive...' You can meet him, and in your own life you can discover who he is.

4

His Son, our Lord

BUT WHAT difference does it make to us?

It makes a very great difference to our understanding of God. You can come to believe in God as Creator and Ruler by meditating about your own life and about the planet and the universe where you live – as so many non-Christians do. You can begin to believe that God's character is like a father's. But even so, you will probably still think that God is very high above you. The difference made by Jesus Christ is that now God is near, and can be called 'Father!' in deep love and happiness.

Amazing as this is, we feel *at one with* God – the old word for which is 'Atonement'. We know God as Father through Jesus Christ. Man meets God through the 'go-between' or, in the old phrase, the 'mediator'. And so Christians find themselves driven by their own experience to make the Christian statement about God. This is the statement that God is not only known as Father, he is also known as Son.

Every man, woman or child ever born is, in a sense, a son or daughter of God the Father. But not everybody has lived a life such as that of Jesus of Nazareth! In fact, no one has come near to repeating that life, let alone doing better than it. The history of the world has not produced a man or a woman to match Jesus. The closest people have got to the standard set by Jesus has been in the lives of the Christian saints – but those saints have, one and all, completely depended on the divine power which (they

29

have said) has come to them through Jesus. That is why all Christians have always maintained that Jesus is *the* Son of God in a special, utterly unique, sense. And that is why, century after century, Christians have struggled to develop theology (a word which means 'reasoning about God') in a Christian way – thinking about God by exploring what is revealed about him in Jesus Christ, his Son.

Although Christian theology, like any other serious subject, has its technical side which is done by the experts, every Christian is under an obligation to think about God in that way – and think hard. For to say that Jesus Christ is *the* 'Word of God' means that his life is the climax of all God's creation – and the clue to the mystery of what God intends by his creation. He is (so to speak) the A and the Z, and now all the other letters can be arranged in order. So our understanding of the whole world is profoundly influenced if we accept the revelation of God's character and purpose in Jesus Christ. We ought to read the newspapers with this in mind. In this light we ought to examine any knowledge we may have of science, or economics, or psychology, or history. We ought to use Jesus as the way to the truth about all life.

And as the way to the truth about the eternal God. While he lived as man for thirty years or a bit more in Palestine, Jesus prayed to his Father, obeyed his Father, walked with his Father into all life's problems and into death. Christians have always seen in that relationship the enfleshment or 'incarnation' of a relationship which goes beyond time and space into eternity. Jesus is eternally the Son. This is the vision which has made Christians feel that it is right to pray not only to God the Father (as Jesus did in Palestine) – but also to Jesus himself, in eternity.

This faith in Jesus, the living Word and the eternal Son of God, involves us personally – for a great difference is made to our lives, if we kneel as Thomas does at the end of John's gospel and say to Jesus: 'My Lord and my God!'

The best way to see this difference is to see what the *death* of Jesus means to us. Often the whole life of a hero or heroine is summed up in the way he or she dies. That is supremely true in the case of Jesus. He accepted a very painful and humiliating death in Jerusalem – when he could easily have avoided any risk by living quietly in Galilee, where he had worked as a carpenter. His willingness to die shows his courage. It also shows his love for his friends. And it shows something more.

It shows the love of God in action. That love was like sunshine, making Jesus grow and work as he did – but, when Jesus was crucified, the love of God was like sunshine going through a magnifying glass. You can easily make that experiment and find out that, in sunshine under a magnifying glass, paper or a leaf burns. The crucifixion of Jesus makes the strong love of God so clear that (so to speak) our hearts are set on fire.

For it is when we see Jesus patiently suffering that we realise how *patient* the love of God is. God has been patient with the earth through the millions of years of evolution – but perhaps he has had to be more patient still with us, in the few years we have been alive. Although God's happiness must be great beyond our understanding, we can begin to understand that the patience involved in God's chosen method of working must be similar in some ways to our own experience of suffering. As Jesus hangs on the cross dying, we begin to see that his acceptance of pain is not only the act of a brave and loving man. It is also a kind of poster, or film, which is about God's love for his whole creation and specially for mankind. And that moves us more than all the majestic power of God displayed in an earthquake or in the stars.

When we see Jesus on the cross, we also begin to see how terribly wrong mankind has been in responding, or failing to respond, to God's good purpose. Jesus was rejected and left alone – as God the Father has often been.

He was treated with contempt and cruelty – and people have often behaved in the same way towards God's creation, specially towards the men and women who are God's children. When we see that happening, we know that if we had been there we should probably have behaved as the cowardly friends of Jesus did, or as the mob did (shouting 'Hosanna' one day and 'Crucify' before the end of the week), or as Jewish priests did, or as the Roman soldiers did. The word 'sin' now has a serious meaning – because *when we realise what people like us did to Jesus, we know what sin does.*

In the old days people pictured 'devils' as causing sin, disease and death. In our time many people find such pictures amusing rather than frightening, and so the old pictures may fail to bring home to us the fact which lies behind them – the fact that evil is very powerful, spreading like poison in the spirit of man, growing like cancer to destroy. In the old days people spoke of 'the sin of Adam'. In our time most people know that the story of Adam and Eve is not literally true – and they have forgotten that in Hebrew Adam meant 'Man' and Eve meant 'Life'. So the old words may not speak to us of the terrible power of evil in the life of man. But the crucifixion of Jesus speaks.

The most wonderful thing about the cross is, however, that it makes us see that *the patient love of God is stronger than the most powerful evil.* For nothing – nothing at all – can defeat God's purpose, which is always to reach us in healing and forgiveness. Just as Jesus on the cross does not change in his spirit while his body dies, so God does not change. Man does his worst – and God carries on being God. Seeing this, we see what matters to us about the death of Jesus.

There are many ways of putting this. Some Christians have spoken of a great victory won on the cross. And that is a true way of speaking. Some Christians have spoken of the sacrifice made by Jesus. And that also is true, for, as a soldier sacrifices his life in order that victory may be possible, so Jesus lays down his life. Some Christians have spoken of Jesus carrying the consequences of mankind's sin. When he is tortured to death as a result of sin, Jesus takes it like a boxer accepting 'punishment' in the ring. Some Christians have spoken of the death of Jesus as our 'redemption' – which means that it is like buying back a man from slavery by paying the price of his freedom (the ransom). So we are freed from slavery under sin. Some Christians have spoken of the appeal of the cross to our consciences. Paul wrote to the Romans: 'Christ died for us while we were yet sinners, and that is God's own proof of his love towards us' (5.8.) And some Christians have spoken of the whole world being bought back to the knowledge and love of God, by seeing God in the crucified Jesus. That is what Paul wrote in his second letter to the Corinthians (5.18, 19): 'From first to last, this has been the work of God. ... God was in Christ reconciling the world to himself.'

There is a technical term which Christians use: *grace*. In ordinary modern speech, the word refers to attractiveness, charm and ease – specially in movement. We speak of an athlete jumping gracefully, or of a graceful yacht. We are liable to forget that God is supremely attractive – and supremely generous. But when we survey the cross where Jesus died, we remember. And then we know what Paul meant when he wrote of 'the grace of our Lord Jesus Christ'.

There is another technical term in the Christian vocabulary: *justification*. This refers to a prisoner who is made just or innocent by a merciful judge – although the prisoner is in fact guilty. Christians feel like this when they trust in the mercy of God after viewing the cross – when they 'believe in' God as they believe or trust in their dearest friend. That is the explanation of what Christian theology says about 'justification by grace, received through faith'.

By dying like that, Jesus has won the right to be 'our

Lord'. The word 'lord' here means 'boss'. This patiently loving master is invited by all Christians into their lives. He enters our lives like a quiet guest. But he stays there to run things if we will let him. He is ready and able to save us from the results of our own foolishness — which is why he has so often been called 'the Saviour'. Anyone can ask him. Anyone can experience his gentle power. But it must be a personal and repeated decision — one by one, day by day.

There are many ways of defining what 'a Christian' is. The best way is this: a Christian is one who takes orders from Jesus Christ as Lord. There are many ways of defining what 'the Church' is. The best way is this: the Church is the fellowship of those who accept Jesus as Lord. And there are many ways of defining what 'man' is. The best way is this: God took human nature to embody his own nature, and that shows the value of man. Those who accept and follow Jesus are acknowledged by him as his brothers and sisters; hearing God speak through him, they are united with him for ever. But everybody — whatever his or her religion, colour, nationality, income, education or beauty — is a brother or a sister in an important sense. They walk the same earth that Jesus walked. They have the same flesh.

In the Church of England's new Communion service (1973), some of the wealth of Christian thought about Jesus is indicated in prayer to God. 'The day of our deliverance has dawned; and through him you will make all things new, as he comes in power and triumph to judge the world . . . He took our nature upon him and was born of the Virgin Mary his mother, that being himself without sin he might make us clean from all sin. . . . He revealed the radiance of his glory, and brought us out of darkness into his own marvellous light. . . . For our salvation he was obedient even to death on the cross. The tree of defeat became the tree of glory; and where life was lost, there life has been restored. . . . By his death he has destroyed death, and by his rising again he has restored to us eternal life.'

Those are some of the things that have been said about Jesus. What more can be said now? It is for a new generation to say.

5

We believe in the Holy Spirit

THE OLD word for Spirit – 'Ghost' – is nowadays misleading. *The Spirit is power for life.*

That is why it is only two-thirds of the truth to say that Christians believe in God the Father and Jesus the Son. The belief that God is Three-in-One, or the Holy Trinity, is based solidly on Christian experience. It stresses the unity of God, for Christianity is utterly opposed to the worship of many gods (whether they are religious or political or commercial). There is only one real God – as there is only one real universe, which is his creation. Do not think for a second that Christianity teaches that there are three gods. But three ways have been shown to us – three ways in which God is God. There is (1) the way in which God makes, keeps and holds together all that exists – as Creator, Ruler and Father. There is (2) the way in which God acts in patient but victorious love, in a human life – as the Son. And there is (3) the Spirit. It is because Christians have had this experience that they struggle to make sense of it, just as a man who is in love tries to speak of that.

The teaching about God as the Holy Trinity has to cover the fact that Christians have experienced the glory of God in all these three ways. None of them is second-rate. So Christians believe that in each way God is being himself personally – although God is not three separate people.

That is why God the Spirit is spoken of as 'he' not 'it' –

although the Spirit is believed to be given by God the Father through God the Son. And that is why Father, Son and Spirit can each be worshipped as fully divine – although Christian prayer is normally offered (1) *to* the Father (2) *through* the Son (3) *in* the power of the Spirit. The activity of God, as experienced by Christians, is summed up by Paul as he ends the second letter to Corinth: 'the grace of the Lord Jesus Christ, and the love of God, and fellowship in the Holy Spirit.' It is an astonishing phrase, for it shows how early in their history the Christians felt themselves compelled by their experience to speak of the Lord Jesus Christ, and of the Holy Spirit, in the same breath as they spoke of God.

In the Bible the activity of God is often compared both with fire and with water. The main point of the comparison is the sheer excitement of knowing that God acts – it is like suddenly seeing a fire in the dark night, or like finding water in the desert. But it may help our understanding of God's action to notice that there are three equally effective ways in which fire is fire. Fire gives warmth – fire gives light – and fire burns. There are also three equally effective ways in which water is water. Water quenches thirst – water washes – and water makes steam, which can supply the energy to run a machine.

This belief that God is Three-in-One is Trinitarian the centre of fully Christian thinking, and it ought to alert us to the significance of God the Holy Spirit. But it is even more vital that we should have the experience which is here being talked about. For only the full Christian experience, including experience of the energy of the Holy Spirit, makes Christianity what it ought always to be – fire in the world, a torrent of living water.

What, then, does God the Holy Spirit do? The Bible gives many answers. The word 'spirit' suggests what is greatest in human activity. When someone is making his or her best effort, there is a phrase which is sometimes used in order to applaud: 'that's the spirit!' So whenever

God is specially active, the Bible speaks about his 'Spirit'.

In the Old Testament the Spirit of God is said to have been over the waters which chaotically covered the earth in an early period (or 'day') of the earth's creation. Out of those waters life came – as modern science agrees. But God's special activity occurs most dramatically in the lives of men and women when at last they, too, are created. The Old Testament says that in many such lives the 'Spirit' is at work. The Spirit of God is said to have inspired the early heroes of Israel who were clever and energetic (the judges), the men and women who later on were Israel's bravest and best guides (the prophets), Israel's wisest rulers (the kings), and the skilled craftsmen and artists who made beautiful furnishings and robes for the temple in Jerusalem. So the Bible applauds the Spirit of God in many places, but chiefly in the spirit of man.

Here in the Bible is a vast picture of the Spirit's work. Our understanding of the world in our time – and of all the past – must not be smaller. Whenever we see something new being created by adventure, and progress being made through taking risks, and reversals or waste being accepted in an unconquerable hope, we should say: 'there's God!' Whenever order emerges out of chaos, and life out of dull matter, we should say: 'that's the Spirit!' Whenever there is in the spirit of man some outstanding ability, such as scientific ability or athletic ability, we should say: 'that's a gift!'

But in the New Testament, a surprising new way of the Spirit's activity is reported – which is why Christians give the Spirit a new honour. What is surprising is that now the most ordinary people, leading the most commonplace lives, are invaded, shaken and possessed by the Spirit. And all this is because of the new man – Jesus.

The new life which floods into Christians is life brought by Jesus, and the new truth which they glimpse is the truth made human in Jesus. Their new power is the power of the Holy Spirit – seen, as never before, in Jesus. Their new prayer is like having a brilliant lawyer or 'advocate' to speak up for one, saying what one could never express so well oneself – but this advocate carries on the work of Jesus.

All this is implied in the thrilling promises of the farewell speech of Jesus in John's gospel (chapter 14). 'I will ask the Father, and he will give you another, to be your Advocate, who will be with you for ever – the Spirit of truth. ... Because I live, you too will live. ... The Holy Spirit whom the Father will send in my name will teach you everything, and will call to mind all that I have told you.'

Jesus, who was so full of the Spirit, promised that the Father would give the Spirit to those who asked, as a parent always gives food to a hungry child who asks. In Jerusalem, when for the first time after the crucifixion and resurrection of Jesus they were celebrating the Jewish harvest-festival called Pentecost, this promise came true. The small company of Christians felt themselves filled with a new power. In their excitement they broke out in strange sounds and cries. They excited those around them, who then listened to the first Christian sermon. And their new power did not leave them. It gave them courage to defy the authorities. It gave them eloquence to announce their message and to argue for its truth. It gave them the power to heal many who were sick. The power of the Spirit was what took the Christian faith from Jerusalem into the whole of Palestine, and gradually into the whole of the world.

The Acts of the Apostles, which tells the story of this Pentecost in its second chapter, is St Luke's account of how the new faith was taken from Jerusalem to Rome, where it proved stronger than the Roman empire itself. That book shows that wherever the faith went, the promise was repeated that the Spirit would be given. And the Spirit came. He came to people of many nations and races. He came to men and women – most of them poor and uneducated, a few of them influential and intellectually brilliant. These Christians still had many human weaknesses – but at least they knew that! Their pride was (as Paul wrote) crucified. For the Spirit always came with a shattering power.

The same power has been experienced by Christians in every generation since those first days. Sometimes intense emotions have been aroused, and the ability to speak in 'strange tongues', as known at that Pentecost festival in Jerusalem, has also been known by many other Christians. Christians who specially value such gifts of the Holy Spirit can be called Pentecostalists, and there are flourishing Pentecostal Churches in the world today. When these Christians remain loyally within Churches such as the Anglican Churches, they are called the 'Charismatic' movement, from the Greek for 'gift'.

But the extraordinary excitements are not the gifts of the Spirit which have been most emphasised in Christianity. The stress has been on the quieter, perhaps longer-lasting, gifts shown in the Christian character. Courageous leaders and spokesmen, wise healers and teachers, generous friends, humble saints – all are Christians given power by God the Spirit. And the Spirit's gift of *love* has been put first, as the most important.

Writing to the Galatians (5.22), Paul described the 'harvest' of the Spirit. Here it is: 'love, joy, peace, kindness, goodness, fidelity, gentleness and self-control.' People sometimes talk as if such virtues can be manufactured, or produced by human effort. But that is not the Christian experience. The reason why all these virtues are called a 'harvest' is that each of them comes from a seed, as does the wheat in the field or the apple on the tree. That seed is God's love for us. As Paul wrote to the Romans: 'God's love has flooded our inmost heart through the Holy Spirit he has given us' (5.5).

Here Christian experience corresponds with our observation of those we meet every day. We notice that people who are self-controlled, gentle, loyal, good and kind are people who are deep in themselves at peace and full of happiness. Those who are loving are those who have been loved – by their parents, by their friends, by their wives or husbands. Because they are assured of love, they have a relaxed and generous attitude to others. But the Christian experience is that even those who have been starved of human love can experience God's love, while those who have known the richness of human love can find that God's love is better. In their hearts, God's Spirit can be poured out lavishly.

This, then, is the third way in which God is God. And when we know this, we are not surprised about what Christians have always said: without the good news of God the Spirit, there is no full account of the Christian message. Nor are we surprised when Christians ask each other: 'have you, too, received the Spirit?' Christianity is sometimes presented as a series of challenges – do better, and better still! But it matters far more that this good news is a series of offers – you need it, so here is strength!

When people eventually realise that the Christian message *is* good news, and that the Spirit has this splendid reality in the lives of so many, they often want to know how they, too, can receive the gift of the Spirit. To that, there is only one possible answer: *you must ask for it*. The Bible is absolutely clear about this, and so is Christian experience. Everyone who asks receives.

6

We believe in love

EVERYONE WANTS to be loved. We rely on the support and approval of our friends. Sex is a big part of human nature, and most of us need the special warmth and companionship of the girl friend or the boy friend, the wife or the husband. We also need the security of a loving home, with a family life based on the rock-like foundation of a stable marriage. Without such love, we are lonely and lost.

But what is 'love'? Obviously, sex is often a vehicle for love. And it is equally obvious that many people think that Christians are unaware of this. Many people suppose that Christianity takes an entirely negative attitude to sex. So it is best to be frank.

Sex is a hunger reminding us that physically we are not far removed from the apes from whom we are descended. But human sex is more than physical – and that is a reminder that we are staggeringly special among the animals. Human sex includes the physical side, which for most people is extremely important and great fun, but the emotional side matters even more. Human sex means a series of thrills, delights and responsibilities which are *all* parts of the most significant activity of the human spirit, love.

Most people while they are growing up (a process which may last until their thirties or until their deaths) find sex a problem. If the physical instinct is to lead to really human sex, we have to develop more self-control than the monkeys, steering this powerful engine towards love – and that's our problem.

Some of the ways in which sex can be a problem are so common that it is only sensible to make sure that everyone understands them. Nowadays we can discuss these matters honestly and frankly. Indeed, there is so much talk about them that people often ask: can anything be called 'right' or 'wrong' any longer? It may help if one Christian now states what he thinks, for others to consider. If it seems that what follows is too dogmatic, please blame it on the need to be brief! Actually, there is only one law: *sex should serve love.*

Our bodies let us know that they are developing sexually. Many young people are troubled by acne, or 'spots'. Young men's voices break; young women have 'periods' every four weeks. There is nothing to be worried about in all this – it is simply the natural way of getting ready to be a father or mother.

Many young people play with their bodies sexually. This 'masturbation' has often been condemned as wrong. Certainly it isn't essential – some people can, and do, grow up happily without doing it. But nowadays it is realised that masturbation does no physical harm, and probably most Christians would say that you should not feel guilty about it, if you feel that you very much want to do it sometimes to get rid of the tensions which build up inside you.

Another result of this physical instinct is that almost everyone – specially when growing up and exploring what sex means – get harmlessly and enjoyably excited about other people's bodies. And this is a step forwards, because it shows us that mature sex is going to be the very opposite of being absorbed in ourselves. Everyone realises how much of pop music refers to sex, and photographs of pretty girls or handsome men mean sex, too. We have fantastic dreams of adventure and success in sex. We may intensely admire someone we know – it may be a boy with

43

a boy or a girl with a girl, or it may be the first wonderful feeling of a man's love for a woman or the other way round.

Some photographs and love stories can remind you that the human body, in addition to being a marvellously efficient machine, is also like a church – for it is the temple or the spirit. Some of the greatest works of art, showing the dignity and glory of being human, are nudes.

There is another kind of material – in magazines, novels and films – which is pornography. There is no happiness in it and there is nothing beautiful or amusing about it. It treats the human body as a butcher treats meat – and this dirt is usually more expensive than meat.

People who find that they are unable to make a partnership in sex and marriage should seek expert help through a doctor because dreams and photographs are no substitute for real sex. People who feel attracted only by their fellow-men (homosexuals) or fellow-women (lesbians) ought also to consult a doctor. Some people can be cured of this, so that they lead a normal life. Others cannot be cured – and they, too, have to learn how to live and love, which they certainly can do. If homosexuals and lesbians cannot be cured, they should not be condemned. They can control themselves so that they aren't a nuisance to people (specially young people) with a normal attitude to sex. They can be happy and respected members of society.

The normal course is to have a number of girl friends or boy friends while we are too young to marry. Such friendships are part of life's happiness – and they help us to prepare for marriage.

One of the things that makes a man is self-control, specially in sex – for one of the things an intelligent, sensitive man learns is that most women enjoy sexual intercourse only if they feel relaxed, secure and loved. You are not respecting a girl if in fact you are running the risk of hurting her physically or emotionally. You are not loving

44

her if you want to use her body as a machine to give yourself thrills.

And if you are a girl, you may get either hurt or coarsened in your emotions if you say 'yes' to the physical side of sex before you are ready for marriage. Don't do it just because he wants to! If he really respects you he will not expect you to hurt and cheapen yourself. And don't believe him if he tells you it would show you if you would be happy married to him. It would show you very little — except that he feels free to have sex with women to whom he is not married.

What matters most is that men and women should honour each other, because real love grows through real respect. That is the most important argument against having sex with your girl-friends or your boy-friends. It is also worth remembering that there is a danger of venereal disease, caught by having sex with someone who already has the disease. Many people catch it nowadays and it can be extremely unpleasant and dangerous, although usually it can be cured if you consult a clinic in time.

As many thousands of unmarried mothers discover in their own bitter experience in this country every year, there is also the danger of having an unwanted baby unless you *always* take *effective* precautions. That is tragically unfair on the baby as well as on the mother, although unmarried women who are pregnant can get help to have and keep the baby. Abortion, which involves having the live foetus which would have become the baby removed and killed before birth, is *not* an operation which a woman can get done easily — and it is *not* a nice experience for the woman, or the surgeon, or the nurse. It is an operation which can be done efficiently and legally — but only when there is a real risk to the physical or mental health of the mother-to-be or the child-to-be. And it is very dangerous to have the operation done by someone who is unqualified and illegal.

Some people always remain unmarried because the

right partner never seems to come along. They often lead very happy lives, particularly if they find satisfying work and many opportunities for being with other people in friendship and service; indeed, in the way they love and care for others they can be far more impressive than a shut-in, selfish married couple. Others remain unmarried through their own choice, because they dedicate their lives to work which could not be done so well if they had responsibilities to a family. These are the 'celibates' – for example, monks and nuns. Their love is often heroic.

Those who are married begin to learn, far more deeply than they ever knew before, what love means. Here are some of the words of the marriage service in church. 'I take thee to my wedded wife, to have and to hold from this day forward, for better, for worse, for richer, for poorer, in sickness and in health; to love and to cherish, till death us do part. ... With this ring I thee wed; with my body I thee honour; and all my worldly goods with thee I share ...'

That is the Christian understanding of marriage, for here are two people giving themselves to each other. Sex before marriage cannot be that. You cannot be married as an experiment to be abandoned when you meet a problem, as you break off a love-affair before marriage. That is not real marriage – it is like getting out if the water seems a bit cold. And until you are married, you cannot tell what it will be like. Just having sex physically will not show you – that is like putting a toe into the water. Real marriage is like diving into a swimming pool. You either swim or you don't – it is your decision. But real marriage is such a big decision that it is madness to rush into it.

A marriage becomes strong as both husband and wife learn to put up with each other's faults and to make each other happy. They become content to sacrifice their own inclinations. Marriage is a steady giving – and it is often hard work. But it is also the most marvellous getting: for the love which is given in marriage is returned – and

46

more. It is the best kind of friendship there is, and no other happiness in this life matches it. Marriage is always changing slightly as time marches on. (For example, nowadays it is normal for wives to work outside the home if they want to or need to, before and after the years given to looking after the children.) But the secret of a happy marriage is always the same: the conquest of selfishness.

That is also the secret of all happiness!

Many advertisements pretend that if you buy something they want to sell, you will be happy. And obviously we all need not only bread but also some other things – we need them physically or emotionally. (It would be interesting to make a list of what you need!) Obviously, too, we all like jam on the bread. Many things are luxuries but we can buy them with a reasonably clear conscience if we have earned the money.

However, the fact – not the theory, but the fact – is that happiness does *not* consist of the number of things we possess. It is possible to be happy with only a few possessions – ask any African! It is possible to be lonely, bored and discontented while rich – look around you in any luxury hotel! We are often told that we need luxurious furniture, food and clothes, as advertised in the glossy magazines. We are also told that we need drugs – 'pot' or the far more dangerous 'hard' drugs, or the more middle-aged drugs of alcohol, tobacco and gambling. And obviously some of these things are fun – in sensible quantities, at prices we can afford. But it is nonsense for the advertisers to promise us happiness in exchange for our money.

The truth is that happiness is much more likely to be found in the mind than in what our money can buy. To learn the secret of happiness, we have to understand the laws which govern our emotions.

One of these laws is that we are happy when we drown our worries in doing something we enjoy. Each of us has worries, and they are often about how we look in the mirror or what people think of us. We have many reasons for condemning ourselves – or being sorry for ourselves. Brooding on these worries gets us nowhere, except perhaps to hell; for 'hell' is self-centred despair. We shall not be happy unless we take a holiday from ourselves, and the easiest way of doing that is to throw ourselves into an activity – which may be cooking, or mending a cycle, or reading, or pretty well anything that demands our attention.

We all know that it is usually more fun to do things with other people. But this doesn't apply only to a family or to a team at sport or to a group of young people. Many older people enjoy their jobs largely because of the friends they find at work – and people who are not out at work miss the companionship as well as the money. Friendship is very obviously the best road to happiness.

Everyone knows that! But nowadays we need to grasp this truth again and again, because so much on TV and in the newspapers seems to be an attempt to make us forget it. TV and the papers are full of violence, real or fictitious. All this must appeal to an aggressive instinct in human nature. Again we meet the animal inside man! At its worst, this material is as filthy and corrupting as any sexual pornography, and the only sensible reaction is to say a similar 'no' to it. Even when it is presented responsibly, the constant emphasis on violence and controversy is depressing and deadening.

Often people who have made their fortunes by cheating, and who had protected their reputations by lying, are held up to us for admiration. But the truth is that they are not the people able to teach us how to be successful. You can get some money by cheating, and you can get some power by lying, but a truly successful man or woman is a happy one – and to be happy you need friends. You will not have friends if you make a habit of cheating or lying. And these are habits easily formed.

But how do you make friends? Many people, specially young people, ask themselves this question and become miserable, locked in the prison of the self, because they don't think they are popular. Yet they are like prisoners with keys in their hands! For we make friends by being friendly. On the whole, people think about us precisely as we think about them. If we dislike them, they adopt the same attitude. If deep down we can't be bothered with them, they won't cross the street to meet us. It is only when we give that we receive. It is those who give love who get it back.

If you ask 'how can I make myself more attractive?' you ought to notice that the really attractive person is usually the one who takes a real interest in other people. If you ask 'what's the answer to all my problems?' you probably need to go out and get to know someone with far greater problems, who will teach you what courage and happiness mean – and will richly repay any friendship you can offer.

When Jesus was challenged to sum up the whole of the moral teaching of the Bible as he knew it, he did not hesitate. He quoted (from Leviticus 19.18): 'Love your neighbour as yourself.' Originally that seems to have meant: 'Stick by your fellow-Jew.' But to Jesus it meant: 'Everyone you meet is your neighbour – put yourself in his place, and give him the love you would want in his place.' The only words of Jesus to be quoted directly by Paul are these: 'Happiness lies more in giving than in receiving' (Acts 20.35) And the only saying of Jesus to be recorded in all four gospels is the warning that the man who saves his life will lose it. Fight your neighbour, and he will fight back! Love, and you will be loved! Fight to keep your self-centredness in your own private life, fight in order to get as much as you can, and you will never know happiness! But give your life to your neighbour, give your life away in love, and you will notice that you are happy when you are too busy to worry about it! That is the secret which Jesus tells.

In his first letter to the Corinthians (chapter 13), Paul created an unforgettable portrait of Jesus Christ – and of the true Christian. It is the portrait of a man who has found his life after apparently losing it because he is so unselfish. He has found his life, because he has found what love can do. 'Love is patient, love is kind and envies no one. Love is never boastful, nor conceited, nor rude, never selfish, not quick to take offence. Love keeps no score of wrongs; does not gloat over men's sins, but delights in the truth. There is nothing love cannot face; there is no limit to its faith, its hope, and its endurance.'

Rightly, that description of love is one of the most popular parts of the Bible. What has been said so far is, however, not the full Christian understanding of love. The advice to treat other people as we should wish to be treated if we were in their shoes is known as the 'golden rule' and it is given in the Bible. But the Bible says much more.

The Bible shows that to believe in love is *to trust in the power of love*. It is to act in the conviction that love will find a way and win through. So many other things seem more immediately attractive than true love, and in this chapter we have already mentioned some of them – sex for kicks, possessions, drugs. But to believe in love is to say that true love is the most valuable, the most satisfying and the most glorious experience in life. It is to say that here is gold – and the rest is bogus. So many other things seem more powerful than love. Violence often does. Aggressive argument often does. But to believe in love is like expecting a great river to flow into the sea. You trust love to win through because it is the mightiest force, the most dynamic energy, in the universe.

How can we believe *that*? It is never easy. In fact, it is only possible if we believe in God the Father – for only if God is real and loving is love more real than the other things. And Christians are those who believe in God as Father because they have seen the Father's love triumphant in the life, death and victory of Jesus, his Son our Lord. This Christians believe because they have been touched by the power of the Spirit. What this chapter has said about love is based, for the Christian, on what previous chapters have said about God.

If we turn to John's first letter in the New Testament, we shall find that the fourth chapter gives very briefly and very simply, but also very profoundly, a Christian account of love.

First, John insists that some education in loving people is needed before we can begin to know and love God. 'Everyone who loves is a child of God and knows God, but the unloving know nothing of God. ... God is love; he who dwells in love is dwelling in God, and God in him.'

Second, John warns us that to wander from the path of love is to lose touch with God, and he is ruthlessly practical about what love means. 'If a man says, "I love God" while hating his brother, he is a liar.'

Third, John emphasises that Christianity is not chiefly about *our* love. Our love for our brothers educates us into loving the loving *God*. 'For God is love; and his love was disclosed to us in this, that he sent his only Son into the world to bring us life. The love I speak of is not our love for God, but the love he showed us. We love because he first loved us.'

Finally, John returns from his little meditation on the divine love to our practical behaviour. 'If God thus loved us, dear friends, we in turn are bound to love one another. Though God has never been seen by any man, God himself dwells in us if we love one another; his love is brought to perfection in us. ... And indeed this command comes from Christ himself: that he who loves God must also love his brother.'

7

We believe in forgiveness

EVERYONE WANTS to stop pretending. We are all failures, and pretending to be successful is a burden. We try to cover up our weaknesses like a woman trying to conceal the blemishes on her face – but even if we deceive others we can't convince ourselves. Particularly do we feel this when we measure ourselves in comparison with the highest standards of love. Our lives are seen to be really sordid when we look at them honestly in the light of that ideal.

Even if we are blind to these facts about our own lives, the state of the world (as this is brought home to us by TV and the papers) is almost bound to make us conscious of the failures of human nature. Instead of cooperating in constructive tasks, groups spend their energies in rivalries which are often bitter. Instead of treating this planet with the respect it deserves, men behave like a bird fouling its own nest. Instead of combining to grow and distribute food for all, some people on this small planet worry about slimming while others worry about starving. And all the time, horror-weapons are kept at the ready with cities as their targets; our civilisation is never more than a few minutes away from the possibility of destruction. The heart of man is such that nuclear missiles grow out of it. Everyone wants to stop pretending that this is an acceptable way of running the world.

It is sometimes said that 'modern man feels no guilt',

but that is true only of the stupid. Anyone who is at all sensitive to what is going on in his or her own mind, or the world around, knows why guilt features so prominently in most religions – and why the instinct of man is to hope that a God exists who will listen to the prayer, 'Lord, have mercy!'

An old prayer says to the Lord Jesus Christ: 'you take away the sin of the world.' It is almost as if we were thinking about a great bulldozer clearing away the ruins of a building and all the mud and muck. When we begin, we are burdened by our many failures as individuals and as the human race. When he has finished, he has removed the whole mess so that it can be forgotten. And when we begin again to make the mess, he begins again to take it away.

What Jesus does here is to express God's mercy in action. Supremely he did this when he continued to embody love despite the loneliness and pain of his death, praying: 'Father, forgive them: they do not know what they are doing.' But frequently this happened as he walked around Palestine. He would meet someone paralysed in spirit and in body – someone unable to move because the burden of failure and guilt was so heavy. Then Jesus would speak and act. And that person would be free, a whole person instead of a cripple. Often in his teaching Jesus would explain what was happening. It was as if a son was going back to his father after making mistakes. That son would begin to say: 'Father ... I am no longer fit to be called your son. ...' But the father would interrupt his confession of guilt, saying to his servants: 'Quick! fetch a robe, my best one, and put it on him; put a ring on his finger and shoes on his feet ... and let us have a feast to celebrate the day.' And even *before* that son had said a word to show that he was sorry, the father would run to meet him, would fling his arms round him, and would kiss him.

Why? Simply and solely because that boy was his

53

father's son – whatever he had done wrong. The Christian commentary on human nature is never entirely gloomy. Christianity says that man is a sinner, in case we haven't read as much in today's paper. But Christianity quickly adds that man is also a creature of great dignity and value, an animal with unique skills and powers, a marvellous and beautiful being with almost unlimited opportunities, already full of goodness, the child of God and in many ways like his Father. Countless times a life began in a man's love for a woman. But Christianity adds that human life as a whole arises out of the love of God, who is man's Creator. So the Father sees. The Father cares. The Father runs. And the Father welcomes home.

A typical prayer about sin – a prayer of 'repentance' or 'penitence' (being sorry) – is included in the Church of England's new Communion service. 'Almighty God, our heavenly Father, we have sinned against you and against our fellow men, in thought and word and deed, in the evil we have done and in the good we have not done, through ignorance, through weakness, through our own deliberate fault. We are truly sorry and repent of all our sins. For the sake of your Son, Jesus Christ, who died for us, forgive us all that is past, and grant that we may serve you in newness of life to the glory of your Name. Amen.'

According to the teaching of Jesus, God's forgiveness is offered to all – on two conditions only. We often read with interest the advertisements which say, 'A free gift!' – and add one or two conditions. How much more should we notice the conditions which are attached to the offer to take away the sin of the world!

The *first* condition is that we should mean what we say when we say that we are sorry. The reason why this is necessary is that unless we are really open to receive what God offers we cannot experience the forgiveness and the newness of life. If we do not mean our 'sorry', it is like saying 'welcome' to a guest – and keeping the front door closed. One of the ways in which Jesus makes clear the dignity of man as the child of God is the insistence, found in many places in the gospels, that God will not force himself on us. God will not break down the door if we decide to keep it shut.

Therefore Jesus warned his hearers very solemnly that 'if anyone speaks against the Holy Spirit, for him there is no forgiveness'. This means that if anyone does not accept that good is good and that truth is truth, he or she cannot be shown the truth and cannot be strengthened in goodness. As the twelfth chapter of Matthew's gospel explains, the warning comes when some of the enemies of Jesus have sneered at his work of healing people, saying that it was inspired by 'Beelzebub prince of devils'.

The *second* condition attached to God's free offer of forgiveness is expressed in the prayer which Jesus gave to his followers. 'Forgive us our sins as we forgive those who sin against us!' This means that we cannot ask for God's forgiveness except to the extent that we forgive those who have wronged us. If we love and forgive our fellow men only a little, we shall be forgiven by God only a little; if we are totally unforgiving, we shall be totally unforgiven. (Jesus warned us of our spiritual danger by telling the story of the man whose debt running into millions of pounds was wiped out at a stroke by an extraordinarily generous king. That man left the king and immediately demanded that a fellow-servant should repay him a debt amounting to only a few pounds. When the king heard about that cruel unfairness, he insisted that the scoundrel should pay him back every penny.) But the reason for this second condition is the same as for the first. If we are ungenerous to our fellow-men, it shows that we do not really understand that God is being generous to us, and so we are not able to accept God's free offer. We are still hoping to defend the old life of selfishness; we cannot let ourselves be invaded by the new life.

If we understand this second condition attached to God's offer, what we have to do is to think of those we most dislike – and pray to God, 'Lord forgive me to the precise extent that I forgive that person!' And obviously this includes people whom we dislike because of our prejudices about colour, nationality, class or religion. We have to acknowledge one and all as human – like ourselves. Just as sinful! But just as lovable! When we trust in God's forgiveness, it is because we believe that he understands why his children have such weaknesses. He knows what handicaps we have inherited, what difficult circumstances we face, what fierce temptations we undergo; he knows our difficulties, because he knows us. But that is the way in which we have to see our brother or our sister – to understand, and to forgive.

Anyone can receive God's forgiveness by asking God sincerely for it – if he or she is firmly resolved to live in love and peace with all. But the Church makes available to us, if we want it, an additional privilege. If we wish to confess our sins out loud before a priest, the priest can advise us about any problems and can assure us of God's forgiveness. Any priest of the Church of England is authorised to hear a confession, and is bound to treat it as absolutely private and confidential. The practice is not compulsory in the Church of England – but many are very grateful that the Church provides this privilege, and they regard it as a great blessing in their lives.

These are the traditional words of the forgiveness or 'absolution', which the priest says after hearing the confession. 'Our Lord Jesus Christ, who hath left power to his Church to absolve all sinners who truly repent and believe in him, of his great mercy forgive thee thine offences: And by his authority committed to me, I absolve thee from all thy sins, in the name of the Father, and of the Son, and of the Holy Spirit. Amen.'

It only remains to be added that *neither the warning nor the offer announced by Jesus is cancelled by death.* It is very difficult indeed to use any pictures or words about what lies beyond death, for all the pictures or words which are available refer to life before death. All we can say is if man is what Christianity says he is – not only a sinner but also unique, beautiful and good, the child of God – then God the Father will not throw him away when he dies like a smoker throwing away the end of a cigarette. God is better, more reliable, than that. What the Bible calls 'eternal life' begins here and now, but it is not brought to an end by the death of the body.

There is a grim side to the teaching of Jesus about life after death, for often in the gospels Jesus warns us that the eternal God will still attach those two conditions to his free offer when we have died. If we are to live with God in his glory, we must ourselves be willing to say 'yes' to him. And we must be willing to live in love.

Jesus speaks about hell, using the traditional pictures familiar to his hearers (pictures of perpetual fires and horrid worms, derived from the smouldering rubbish dump in the valley outside Jerusalem). What 'hell' means is saying 'no' to God, preferring darkness to light, hatred to love, death to life. Hell is man's selfishness in eternity. Jesus warns that it is a terrible possibility. But it is also possible that everyone will in the end choose God, light, love and life. Indeed, many Christians believe that this will be the end of the human story – and all Christians hope so.

'Heaven' is God's forgiveness in eternity. The pictures of winged angels, harps, jewels and gold cannot be true literally, for the truth of what is beyond space and time, in God's own life, must be more splendid than any pictures or words. But these pictures, and the great words still used in Christian worship, can point to the reality – as the small models may give an idea of the yacht. What matters about heaven to Chrisians is that, out of what he has himself made, God will make the best that is possible to him. Christians who believe in God, and pray to

him, and try to obey him in their lives, are confident of
God's future because of what they have learned about
God already. They have glimpsed God's glory, and this
makes them hope for the vision of God as he really is in
his eternal perfection. They have experienced God's
faithfulness and loyalty in their lives, and this makes
them long to know God's full love. They trust God to take
care of the ultimate future – and they leave it to him.

We know almost nothing about heaven. But if you believe that God is real, and is your loving Father, then you
can know that he will keep *you* in eternal life – it will be
the same you! And if you believe that God is eternal, and
is holy and perfect, then you can know that you will have
to be changed in order to share his life and his glory – it
will be a completely grown-up you! And what you hope
for yourself you can hope for those who are dear to you –
and for everyone.

A prayer which is often used at funerals expresses this
faith and this hope: 'O Father of all, we pray to thee for
those whom we love, but see no longer. Grant them thy
peace; let light perpetual shine upon them; and in thy
loving wisdom and almighty power work in them the
good purpose of thy perfect will; through Jesus Christ
out Lord. Amen.'

If this is the reality behind our pictures of heaven, then
the hope of reaching it is a great hope inspiring our present struggles. Those whom we call 'saints' are those who,
we believe, have been made perfect by God in heaven. We
believe this because already before death their lives were
special. They were not perfect then, but they showed so
many signs of being in touch with God that they helped
us to trust in God's wisdom and power.

The thought that saints in heaven can be made out of
people like us is gloriously encouraging – a point made in
the New Testament by using two comparisons with ath-
letics in Ancient Greece.

At the sports, a runner who won a race would be

crowned with a wreath made of leaves, and in his first letter to the Christians in Corinth (9.24–26), Paul urged them to aim at a far more valuable prize. 'At the sports all the runners run the race, though only one wins the prize. Like them, run to win! But every athlete goes into strict training. They do it to obtain a fading wreath; we, a wreath that never fades.'

In the letter to Hebrews (chapter 12), the victorious heroes of faith are compared with the spectators who shout encouragement to the competitors at the sports. So we must 'run with resolution the race for which we are entered, our eyes fixed on Jesus'. If some favourite sin of ours is hindering us like an overcoat on a runner, we must stop clinging to it. We must throw it away, as an athlete removes his everyday clothes in order to be free.

8

We believe in freedom

EVERYONE WANTS to be free. A great part of the history of the twentieth century has consisted of the struggle of peoples to be liberated from empires – and from tyrannical governments in their own countries. A cry for freedom has started off the roar of many revolutions. But the history of our time is also the story of a psychological liberation. People rebel against being told what to think and what to do. They demand freedom to work out their own beliefs, to vote for their own spokesmen, to decide how they choose to live, to behave as they think right. In many periods of history young people have rejected the merely conventional – but they are doing it with greater power today, because their revolt chimes in with the general passion for freedom.

Religion is often said to be the enemy of freedom. We are told that Churches and other religious bodies have got themselves identified with imperialism and with oppressive governments. We are told that religion is itself 'opium for the people', a drug used by oppressors to distract people from their just grievances. We are told that preachers become censors when they get the chance, and that religion tries to strangle the free life of the mind and the heart.

Nowadays any honest reply to this criticism of religion has to begin by admitting with sorrow and shame that much of the criticism is true. Religion *has* often been used by those who have oppressed and exploited others. But

60

Christians would now agree that this was tragically wrong. The persecutions of heretics which in the past were officially sponsored both by the Roman Catholics and by the Protestants are now condemned throughout the Christian Church. Christians now reject the kind of mixture or religion and politics that led to the Church of England being so much under the thumb of Tudor monarchs while Roman Catholics were put to death because they were traitors (ordered by the Pope to overthrow Elizabeth I). Everywhere it is acknowledged that the only right policy is religious liberty, and that the Church's role in society is to be a servant not a lord, the pioneer of authentic love rather than the tool of power politics.

The real question is whether Christianity is essentially hostile to freedom. And the answer shouts at us from the Bible. John's gospel (8.32) contains the promise: 'You shall know the truth, and the truth will set you free.' In other words, Christianity originally did not rely on any support offered by the state or by 'respectable' opinion. In the days when it was being persecuted, and was rejected by the respectable, Christianity simply relied on being true – and the way by which people were to know its truth was by finding out for themselves its liberating power.

One of the earliest documents included in the New Testament is Paul's letter to the Galatians. One great theme of that letter is freedom. 'Christ set us free, to be free men' (5.1). The same theme runs through Paul's other teaching. For example, his second letter to the Corinthians proclaims that 'where the Spirit of the Lord is, there is liberty' (3.17).

St Paul – like Jesus himself – contrasted this new freedom with the burden of trying to keep all the laws of strict Jewish religion. But the original freedom in Christianity should also be contrasted with the claims of some *Christian* teachers. For example, in the Middle Ages the Church did its utmost to insist on certain beliefs and

61

practices. These were nowhere to be found in the Bible, yet they were claimed to be essential. The sixteenth century saw the 'Protestant' protest against all this. In our time the bitter controversies of the sixteenth century are dead almost everywhere. But while Protestantism has changed as Roman Catholicism has done, there is a sense in which its position is permanently valid. Anyone who wishes to be loyal to the Christianity of the New Testament always has to protest against any attempt to substitute a man-made code of discipline, in belief or behaviour, for the original Christian freedom.

The belief in freedom is illustrated by the attitude of the Anglican Churches to their own clergy. Anglicanism has no equivalent to, the Roman Catholic doctrine (defined in 1870) that the Pope is, when teaching on faith or morals *ex cathedra* ('from his throne'), 'infallible' (not liable to make any mistake). Nor does it have any equivalent to the Roman Catholic insistence on the confession of sins to a priest. Any member of an Anglican Church is free to disagree with his bishop or with any other teacher – and is free to confess his sins to God without going to any priest. In fact, for many years Anglicanism has been famous for the variety of opinions held by its members about theology and morality – and famous, too, for the freedom with which its members have voiced their opinions without fear. That is still the Anglican character, and those who belong to the Anglican Church accept a certain amount of confusion as the price of freedom.

The reason why Christianity is a message of freedom, and why Anglicanism has had this specially strong belief in freedom, needs to be stated with the enthusiasm it deserves.

A religion is effective *when it is thought to be true*. And you can think it is true when – and only when! – you are free to make up your own mind about it. A compulsory acceptance of orthodoxy is not genuine acceptance. To decide, each individual has to use his or her own reason

62

and conscience – his or her own intelligence, store of knowledge, and moral sense. It is not claimed that either the reason or the conscience is infallible, but in no other way can the individual be convinced. Truth breathes in the air of liberty.

And a religion is effective *when it is personal*. It cannot be personal unless each individual has the freedom to use it in order to approach and serve God in his or her own way. This may not be the same way as the next person's, but the next person has no right to judge and condemn. This is true even if the next person is the Pope! We are free to criticise each other, but we should always remember that a mature attitude to morality must always be based on a person's own decisions. Those decisions may seem mistakes to us – but by taking them, that person developed as a person with his or her own moral sense. Just as religious truth must become *your* truth, so true goodness must be *your* choice.

A careful reading of the New Testament shows great differences among the twelve men first called by Jesus to follow him. It also shows a considerable variety of outlook among Christians and among Christian congregations. One result is that there are four gospels, not one. If you read a letter by St Paul, and then the letter of St James, you might be forgiven for wondering whether the same religion is being described. In Paul's letter to the Galatians, he recalls a fierce argument with Peter: 'I opposed him to his face, because he was clearly in the wrong' (2.1.1). The religion of the New Testament was not uniform, and there is no good reason why Christianity today should be.

Does this mean that truth is never established, that sufficient agreement is never reached about what is right and wrong? Not at all! The New Testament is in favour neither of intellectual laziness nor of practical chaos.

What happens in the Church, as in any other free and healthy society, is that much agreement can be reached by a slow process of careful thought and free debate. It is for this reason that the Church of England arranges for each congregation to meet for business at least once a year, and for the day-to-day life of the Church to be settled after free discussion in the Parochial Church Council and in various higher councils or 'synods'. But even when a majority has been reached, individuals who disagree are not expelled or punished.

Does this mean that every slogan is sacred, or that the purpose of church life is to provide an audience to hear everybody ventilate his or her own pet theories? Not at all! The New Testament attacks the kind of human stupidity and pride that begins: 'What I always say is . . .'

We are all familiar with the fact that sincere religion can do more than anything else to rescue someone from the destructive forms of sex, alcohol, drugs or gambling; from contact with a power greater than himself or herself, someone who had been the slave of a health-wrecking habit gets the strength needed to break free. But it is also a fact that in less dramatic ways *religion can liberate the mind,* for someone who is open to what God wants is delivered from slavery to fashion. There are fashionable opinions just as there are fashionable clothes – and one's mind can be chained to the latest trend. 'Everybody does it' or 'my friends all say so' or 'it was in that paperback' or 'it was on TV' or 'it's the "in" thing' is often said, but it is just not a good enough reason why a Christian should hold an opinion. Humility under God frees a Christian from depending on the crowd's applause.

Christianity can make a big improvement in people's dealings with each other, freeing them from pride. But Christianity is even more interested in the thoughts which people have when they are on their own. Many of us when alone have to wrestle with emotions which carry no prestige – worries, deep anxiety, regrets, guilt, shame, loneliness, a fear that we have been rejected, a sense that our lives are futile and meaningless. The fact that many people when alone feel close to despair is one of the main reasons why so many people need tranquillisers or are mentally sick, amid the luxuries of an affluent society. It is not a new fact – these emotions have always been parts of being human. And to us in this condition, freedom has been announced.

The New Testament's teaching that we are 'ransomed' from 'sin' by the 'blood' of Christ may seem remote from our age, but actually it is that offer many are looking for. 'Ransomed' means liberated. In our time kidnapped people are freed when a ransom has been paid; and in the Roman empire a slave was freed when someone paid his owner the appropriate ransom-money. 'Sin' means everything in us that refuses to accept our own proper dignity in the home of God our Father. The 'blood' of Christ means his life, poured out in love. So the Christian message is that we are liberated from our self-imposed exile, freed into the life with God through life with Christ.

This message offers personal liberation at a level deeper than politics – and the offer was never needed more than in our time, when millions of people who are 'free' (and who in many cases have money and privileges enough and to spare) still feel imprisoned in the cage created for the human spirit by materialism and selfishness. So many of us today are like people who, in release from one prison, immediately head for another – just to be with other prisoners. Christianity calls out each individual to stand undressed before the cleansing forgiveness of God, as a solitary swimmer can stand on the beach at the edge of the sea.

That is why everyone is challenged to respond to God through Jesus Christ in *a personal turning* (which is what the word 'conversion' means). You have to meet Jesus yourself, and to accept him as your friend and as your Lord. You must be able to say for yourself that you believe in him. As Paul's second letter to Timothy (1.12) puts it: 'I know who it is in whom I have trusted.' In the

Church of England's new Baptism service, a question is put. It is very simple, but very searching. 'Do you turn to Christ?' And the Christian is the one who answers: 'I turn to Christ.' If the cost seems too great, remember what the old Anglican prayer says – to serve God as a Christian is 'perfect freedom'. To turn to Christ is to turn to the Liberator.

In many Christian lives, this turning or conversion reaches a climax which can be dated. People can remember the exact time when they accepted Jesus Christ as Lord and Liberator, often after intense struggles to escape from the pressure of his love. But it is not necessary to be able to date your conversion like that. Other Christians reached the position which they now occupy quietly and gradually, without any great conflict in their emotions and without any decisive crisis.

What *is* essential is that everyone should have his or her own personal reasons for being a Christian. You cannot inherit Christian faith as you can inherit red hair or a peculiar nose. You cannot copy Christian faith as you can copy hair style or an accent. And you cannot get it completely out of books, as you can get a knowledge of history. Your faith, to be authentic, to guide your life, must be your own. Your very own experience, whether it is dramatic or quiet, long or short, must lead you to know Jesus Christ as your personal Liberator.

It is instructive to read through the first ten chapters of Mark's gospel (for example), noting how personal were the demand and the offer made by the Liberator. To Simon Peter and Andrew: 'Come with me, and I will make you fishers of men.' To a man with a bad skin disease: 'Be clean again!' To a man who seemed paralysed: 'Stand up, take your bed, and go home.' To a tax-collector: 'Follow me.' To a man with a withered arm: 'Stretch out your arm.' To a man convulsed in fits: 'What is your name?' To a woman in a crowd: 'My daughter, your faith has cured you.' To a little girl apparently dead:

'Get up, my child.' To his disciples: 'And you, who do you say that I am?' To all the people: 'Anyone who wishes to be a follower of mine must leave self behind, he must take up his cross, and come with me. Whoever cares for his own safety is lost, but if a man will let himself be lost for my sake and for the Gospel, that man is safe. What does a man gain by winning the whole world at the cost of his true self?' To the father of a boy who seemed mad: 'Everything is possible to the one who has faith.' And to a rich young man who was dissatisfied: 'One thing you lack: go, sell everything you have, and give to the poor, and you will have riches in heaven, and come, follow me.'

There have been countless women among the friends of Jesus. It is interesting how different are the women who come into personal contact with Jesus in the first ten chapters of Luke's gospel: his own mother Mary and Elisabeth her cousin, Anna in her eighties, Simon Peter's mother-in-law who is ill in bed, the widow grieving for her son in Nain, Mary of Magdala 'from whom seven devils had come out', Joanna the wife of an official at Herod's court, 'Susanna and many others,' Martha so busy with the cooking, Mary her quietly attentive sister. No wonder that Luke tells us (24.10) that some women stayed with Jesus until his death and burial – 'Mary of Magdala, Joanna, and Mary the mother of Jesus, with the other women'!

Then notice at the end of John's gospel the last words of Jesus to Simon Peter. 'Do you love me? . . . Follow me.' Those words are the Christian's invitation to the most wonderful adventure in freedom.

9

We believe in listening

USUALLY WE don't really listen. Radio or TV is a background noise. We meet too many people to think it possible to listen to what they are saying with the kind of attention that catches what they mean but can't say. But many of us want more peace in order to listen more. Sometimes we have *listened* to music – or to friends sharing their secrets. There have even been times when we have listened to trees – or to silence. Those were moments when we were freed from the noisy, futile round-about of our own worries, desires and jealousies.

People who patiently practise it find *prayer* to be the best, most instructive, most calming, encouraging and liberating, kind of listening.

The trouble is that so many people with only a superficial knowledge of prayer think that it is mostly talking. Indeed, they sometimes seem to think that it consists of sleepily repeating the formula: 'God-bless-Mum-and-Dad-and-make-me-a-good-boy/girl.' To such people prayer, even when it is made in adult language, is like telephoning. One pours out many apologies and explantations about oneself, then one produces a long shopping list of things one wants. A phone call like that is so full of our own noise that we doubt whether there is anyone listening at the other end – particularly when we count the things that arrive and find that they aren't exactly what we ordered.

Real prayer is listening to God. The first essential is to 'shut the door', as Jesus put it. The world is very busy, agitating our feelings and exhausting our energies – but here and now, as we begin real prayer we deliberately shut the world out. I am so deeply interested in myself and in how special I am that I can't decide quite what is most interesting about me – but here and now, as I turn to God, I deliberately forget myself. This is to be a journey inwards, but not in order to talk to myself. Real prayer *begins* by concentrating on God. And often it can usefully *end* there!

There is an ancient phrase still used in Christian worship: 'Lift up your hearts!' We have to let ourselves *rise* to the greatness of God – and if need be, we must jump! We enjoy spending time with someone we love; we enjoy just being silent, together. Now we are with God! In the stillness is power, peace, love! But most people find it difficult to use abstract ideas in order to get near God. You may be helped more by looking at a reproduction of a painting, or at a flower. Best of all, gaze on the beauty of God by using the picture of himself which he has supplied: Jesus Christ. Recall to yourself a glimpse of Jesus – teaching, healing, dying on the first Good Friday, rising at the first Easter. That is the likeness of the invisible God.

Normally we read as quickly as possible, because we are reading newspapers, light fiction, business letters, technical publications or textbooks. Or when we are studying a subject, we read as critically as possible. For a change, try reading suitable parts of the Bible as *lovingly* as possible – lingering over the scene, noticing every detail as if you had been there, asking what it shows you of God. Such 'meditation' on the Bible supplies a solid basis for prayer – and life.

When you have got clearer in your mind the reality of God, coming to you in Jesus, stepping out of the pages of the Bible, you will find it easier to put together the jigsaw puzzle of your life. You will want to admit what a muddle your life has been. The pattern of your life can't be seen from the bits – unless someone has caught sight of the picture now broken up into those bits. But even more than that you will want to give thanks for the pattern which is there all the time. The advice to 'count your blessings' is an old recipe for a glad heart, because when bit by bit you lay before God what's right in your life (and in the world's) you will find that what's wrong is reduced to its proper proportions. Most of us have a natural tendency to concentrate on what's wrong – on the problems and grumbles. Prayer is vital if we are to lift up our hearts to the goodness that, as a matter of fact, surrounds us. It is like looking out of the window on a summer's day.

It may help to remember ACT: Adoration, Confession, Thanksgiving. Then – if you have any time left – remember your needs. But do so before God, which makes it different from a supermarket. Jesus encouraged his followers to be thoroughly natural when talking to their Father. Anything that a Christian can rightly want, he can rightly pray for. But there are some practical points to bear in mind.

1. The words which end many prayers in church, 'through Jesus Christ our Lord', are not just a signal to the congregation to add *Amen* (which means 'We agree! So be it!'). They are words reminding us that Christian prayer is prayer which reflects the teaching and character of Jesus Christ. (If we mutter 'grant that my enemy may slip on a banana skin', that is not prayer through Jesus Christ!) These words also remind us that Jesus Christ is the only human being who has ever been thoroughly satisfactory in God's eyes. So Christian prayer is prayer which says to God: 'I know I am human – but so is Jesus Christ! And what I ask is to be made like him!'

2. All that we need to ask for ourselves or for anyone else is that God's will may be done. We should never attempt to dictate to God.

3. Often what we need most is guidance about what God's will is. We can get this guidance by listening. But it

is easy to imagine that some wish of our own has been inspired by God. It is necessary to test what we think is guidance by comparing it with the character and teachings of Jesus Christ as recorded in the Bible.

4. We rightly pray for our physical *needs*, not for luxuries. We ask God for daily bread, not hourly cake.

5. We state needs which God knows already, just as a human parent knows that the children need bread (plus love and some fun). Why, then, ask? For the same reason that it is our duty and our pleasure to use the word 'please' at table. Probably the same food will arrive anyway, but things go better with some courtesy.

6. God normally answers our needs through the natural processes of the world he has provided, and that means that we must do our share in co-operating with him. It is no use praying for the weeds to disappear if we will not get our hands dirty. It is no use praying for distinction in an exam if we refuse to work.

7. God is free to say 'no'. That can be the best kind of answer to prayer – as we learn after a time.

Anything that we can rightly want for ourselves, we shall naturally want for our friends; and anything we want for our friends we can mention to God. Praying for our families and friends is one of the best possible expressions of our love for them. It simply means remembering them and their needs before God. While the whole point of prayer is that *God's* will (not ours or theirs) may be done, you will find that when you have prayed for people you will have a more loving attitude to them as you meet them. Your prayer has not only shown your care – it has deepened it.

Anything we want for our friends we want for those who have a claim on our active sympathy because they have to face suffering – either in the body or in the mind. So we remember before God people who are sick in hospital or at home, people who undergo the bitter experiences of loneliness and despair, and people whose lives have been devastated by violence or some other disaster. This prayer for God's world puts the world where it belongs – in God's hands. But you will find that just as prayer for your friends deepens your friendship, so prayer or 'intercession' for the world strengthens your caring about it.

After praying, you will want to find out whether you can help anyone who is sick or lonely, and how you can fight poverty and war. You will feel more responsible, more involved, more eager.

After being involved in other people's problems, or in trying to do something about the world's giant problems, you are likely to feel tired and depressed – for the problems are complicated, people can be awkward, the tragedies of the world can be completely overwhelming. Then you will want to go back to God in prayer, leaving the problems with him for a time before you begin your own work again. You will find that you need to be told again and again by your Father that you are not to feel responsible for everything. God alone carries the whole burden of what goes wrong – and you can watch him doing it on the cross. And then you will find that you can take up your duties again refreshed, co-operating with God.

Is it necessary to do all these things in order to be any good at prayer? No! These points are merely suggestions which others have found useful. They are *not* meant to make you feel guilty. It is for you to find your own way of praying. One of the wisest things ever said about prayer was this: 'pray as you can, don't pray as you can't.' But it helps to remember also that what is our way of praying at one stage in our lives may not be so satisfactory at the next stage. Our circumstances change, our personalities develop – and so should our prayers. For no one can say before death that he or she has reached the end of the road of prayer. No, when it comes to praying we are all beginners.

Is it necessary to kneel when praying in private? No! Kneeling is a traditional gesture of respect, but you can pray sitting or standing – millions of Christians have done so. Find out what bodily position helps you most. Almost everyone finds it easier to pray with eyes shut, but even this is not essential. You may find it helpful to begin your prayer by taking some deep breaths. They help us to relax and to remember that our prayer is (so to speak) made deep down in us by God as Spirit.

Is it the big thing to 'say your prayers' every morning and every night? No! Remembering God before you begin the day's work, and again before you sleep, clears the mind as a good paste cleans the teeth. The alternative is often to begin the day in a rush and to go to sleep worrying – and both habits are extremely bad for our spiritual health. But many people under modern conditions find themselves with too many things to do in the morning to be able to meditate calmly. Last thing at night, they are tired out. Quiet *listening* is far more important than 'saying your prayers' like a catalogue, and the most practical method may be to set aside some other time to listen to God – for example, early in the evening. It is best to do this every day. But once a week is better than once a month, and once a month is better than never.

Is prayer hypnotising yourself? No! It often suggests things for us to do or be which are not what we should suggest if we were interested only in our comfort. And very seldom does it produce any great emotion. Often it is hard work, and persevering in it when there are so many distractions is a major test of one's character and will-power. Prayer is like tuning in the radio, trying to get rid of interferences and rival programmes.

Is prayer escapism? No! It is the best way there is of getting inspiration and energy for our work – and it is the best way of sorting out our activities so that the peace of prayer gradually controls them all. What goes on in the time and place set aside for prayer ought to be – and can be – related very closely to what goes on in the rest of our lives. Indeed, it ought to – and can – express our lives, because it is no use praying one thing and living another. And our lives ought to – and can – express our prayer, because to work is to pray when we have first concentrated on prayer. Nowadays many people use if not perfume then at least a deodorant. Prayer is the perfume or deodorant of our sweaty existence.

All through the day we have opportunities to turn to God again and (as it were) shoot up 'arrow' prayers. You can pray on a bus, in a kitchen, by a machine, at a desk. *Good God! My God! Thank God!* Even these phrases, usually used without any real thought of God, can be silent prayers. So can the name *Jesus.* The Christians of Russia (and elsewhere) have for many centuries repeated what is called the 'Jesus Prayer'. 'Lord Jesus Christ, Son of God, have mercy on me a sinner.' We are naturally keen on breaks for tea or coffee – but these breaks to recall or 'recollect' the presence of God are at least as refreshing.

Prayer does not change God. Indeed, the whole point of prayer is to remember that God never changes in his attitude to us and to the world. God's attitude is constantly, faithfully, the attitude of love, and it produces a definite plan for us. This plan offers guidance to us – and strength to act accordingly. In obeying that plan lies our hope; in God's will is our peace. Sometimes obedience takes all the courage we have – and more. That 'more' we get through prayer. In the garden of Gethsemane, when Jesus knelt and sweated in an agony, he asked God that he might be spared the crucifixion. '*Abba,* Father, all things are possible to thee; take this cup away from me.' But his natural feelings were controlled and calmed by the prayer: 'Thy will be done!' And he went to the cross.

Prayer does not change God. Prayer changes us.

10

We belong to the Church

THERE IS no such person as a solo Christian. We need groups to make most kinds of music – and families to grow up in – and meetings, movements and political parties to spread opinions – and organisations ranging from a farm to a nation to feed, dress, house, educate, heal, defend and entertain us. And to be Christians, we have to get together.

Perhaps the easiest way of saying what the Church really means is to say this: it is the group which helps us to listen to God. The last chapter discussed prayer as a conversation between God and you-by-yourself. And it was important to discuss prayer like that, because Christianity does offer you the immense privilege and happiness of being able to talk confidently and intimately with God your Father. So you are missing a highly enjoyable and strengthening experience if you never let yourself be alone with him. But many of us find that it is difficult to be alone with God for very long. It isn't only that we are so busy. Another and better reason is that we find prayer easier in a group. Young people sometimes sit cross-legged on the floor in a circle, for a time of quiet which may be all that happens – or which may lead into a few quiet things being said by members of the group. Believe it or not, that is the Church! For here is a group listening to God through Jesus Christ.

Such quiet groups can be so helpful that people ask: isn't that all that is needed? But there is a danger facing any group which meets in private. It may become inward-looking, absorbed in its own group-life. It may become resentful when others try to join it – if they know when it meets and how to join. Experience shows how necessary it is to have a meeting that is *public* and *regular*, in addition to any private groups there may be. And to be practical, in a climate such as Britain's that usually means meeting in a public building.

It is often said: 'You can be a good Christian without going to church.' That is true in two ways. People who aren't regular churchgoers often have attitudes, and do actions, which are approved in the teaching of Jesus. It is also true that clergymen have often exaggerated the importance of church buildings, church services, church organisations and church pronouncements. The State, not the Church, nowadays runs most schools, welfare services and entertainments. Much of the charitable work that is done in our society is not organised by the Church. Television has more influence than preaching. In modern life, the role of the Church has been cut down.

But that is not to say that it would be desirable to abolish the Church altogether. *For what do we mean by 'the Church'?* The Church does not consist of church buildings. In the New Testament the Church flourished – and did not possess a single building. The Church does not consist of ceremonies or doctrines as if it were a cloud in the air. The Church is people! And the Church does not consist of its leaders. Over ninety-nine per cent of the Church consists of lay people! The Church is those Christians who in a particular time and place are willing to stand up and be counted. The end of the Church would mean the end of that.

So far from deserving to be abolished, the Church as God's people deserves to be strenthened – with muscle, not fat. For the Church is the Christian idea in a body, at work. No doubt the idea is more valuable than the Church, just as a man's spirit is more valuable than his flesh – but to survive on the earth the spirit needs the flesh, and to survive in a world which is full of rival ideas the Christian idea needs to be embodied in the Christian society.

It is not good enough to be in favour of Christianity as one supports a football team from an armchair in front of a TV set. Football is kept going because some people play football. Christianity has survived because of the Church and in spite of the many failures of the Church. If you doubt that, ask whether you could have become a Christian yourself had the Church never existed. Most people are attracted to Christianity by the personal example of other Christians – parents, teachers, friends, Christians met in daily life, or Christians known about from the present or the past. But that means that most Christians become Christians because they meet the people who are the Church!

Sometimes people who read the Bible are converted to Christianity just by that, but we still have to ask: who wrote the Bible, who divided it into chapters and gave it titles, who arranged for it to be a book available to that person, who could discuss with that person the full meaning of the Bible? Sometimes people who listen to the radio or watch TV are converted by that, but we have to ask: did the people who made the radio or TV programme rely entirely on other programmes for all their own knowledge of Christianity? Sometimes people have a sudden conviction that Christianity is essentially true – perhaps when they are walking alone. But we have to ask: how did they know what Christianity was? Sometimes people have a vision of Christ. But we have to ask: how did they recognise him? And our questions drive us back to the fact that in the plan of God Christians are made by each other, as fire is spread.

The spreading of the good news of Jesus Christ is called 'evangelism'; the word comes from the Greek for 'good news'. We are ourselves Christians because other people have been evangelists to us. But we do not really believe that it is *good* news if we make no effort to spread it to others. If we sincerely accept it, then we find ourselves challenged to be evangelists.

To whom are we sent as evangelists? Obviously, first to those nearest to us. But if we believe that Christianity means good news to ourselves and to our neighbours, we shall hope that it may be taken everywhere. And so we believe in the 'Catholic' Church, for the word 'Catholic' comes from the Greek meaning 'the whole world'. The Catholic Church is the Christian group which knows that because its news is for everyone, its mission should not be narrower than the world. Any group which intends to be less than Catholic is a hole-in-the-corner affair.

There are plenty of critics who delight in pointing out what is wrong and weak in the Church. But you have to ask yourself how you are linked to the lifetime of Jesus of Nazareth (about the year 30: no one knows the exact dates of the birth and death of Jesus). You have to picture the line of men and women across the centuries reaching you. Some were executed because they were Christians – men such as Andrew, now patron saint of Scotland, and George, now patron saint of England. Others faced great journeys and dangers in order to spread their faith in frightening places – such as Scotland and England. Others met unpopularity and had to overcome many obstacles. Others struggled with many doubts and disappointments. But all these kept the faith and passed it on so that it might be yours. And when Christians refer to the 'communion of saints', they mean fellowship with these people and millions like them – a fellowship stronger than death.

Or picture the Christians around the globe today. Christianity is more fully world-wide than any other religion has ever been, and the Church is the most international body in existence with a large membership.

Some Christians, across the Atlantic or the North Sea,

are richer than you. Some are much poorer, as in India or in the islands of the Pacific. Some are very powerful. Others have to live under many attacks from their government, as in Russia or China. Some are honoured thinkers. Others have to be Christians in countries where most of the public references to Christianity consist of hostile propaganda. Some live in countries which have been 'Christian', at least in name, for fifteen hundred years. Others live in continents which St Paul did not know existed. Some meet in churches which are among the world's chief architectural treasures. Others meet in huts or in the open air, as in an African village. This is the group, family or movement to which you can belong.

All this immense company of people has shared one wish, although many other wishes have clashed with it. It is the wish expressed by an English saint, Bishop Richard of Chichester who died in 1253, in his prayer to see Jesus more clearly, and to love him more dearly, and to follow him more nearly.

They have seen him in each other. Often Christians have received from other Christians such understanding, forgiveness, acceptance, loyalty and friendship that they have through that experience understood more deeply what Christ's love is. And often Christians have seen in other Christians such patience, modesty, self-sacrifice, perseverance, courage and heroism that they have had a firmer faith in Christ's victory. And often Christians have seen in other Christians such a willingness to serve others (usually without any kind of publicity) that they have realised afresh how the love of Christ reaches out victoriously into all the suffering of the world. And often Christians have sensed that other Christians live very close to God, so that they have felt drawn themselves into the new relationship with the Father which Christ made possible.

Probably every group of Christians includes members who are struggling rather than winning in the achievement of this quality of life. If you are able to, help them! But there is no Christian group in the world today, or in history, which would not teach you something about Christ. And in most places where you are likely to go, you will find such a group ready to welcome you.

Unless it is shared with others, and unless it is exposed to the problems involved in living and talking with others, a man's (or a woman's) religion can be very selfish and very much mistaken. That is forgotten by the many people who smugly thank God that they are morally superior to the churchgoers. The remedy lies in thinking of the Church as the 'Body of Christ'. The Christian group is an instrument by which Christ continues his work in the world. It is also a body by which Christ still makes his character known. The man who first called the Church the 'Body of Christ' was St Paul. He used that bold description because on the road from Jerusalem to Damascus he was overwhelmed by the conviction that to damage the Church, as he was doing, was to kick against Christ himself.

And if that is the down-to-earth truth about the Christian religion, then we have to do something practical. Just as it is not enough to play a musical instrument for our own pleasure without ever facing the challenge of joining other music-makers and facing an audience, so it is not enough to have pleasant thoughts on our own about God or about Jesus or about love – if these thoughts are not tested and strengthened by an experience shared with others.

The decisive step to take in joining the Body of Christ is to be baptised. And if we have never really asked ourselves what our membership of the Christian group means, the best way of deepening our understanding is to think more carefully about the meaning of Baptism. It is something more than merely pouring a little water on a baby's head, or making a converted adult take a dip in a stream.

Baptism means the washing away of all that was wrong in the past. In the first Christian century, when 'Gentiles' (non-Jews) wished to accept the religion of the Jews – as many did – they were baptised. John the Baptist, the cousin and announcer of Jesus, insisted that Jews themselves were sinners in need of baptism. Jesus himself was baptised by John in the river Jordan. And the followers of Jesus used the same method to receive both Jews and Gentiles who, confessing their sinfulness, wished to become Christians.

The new Christians accepted the name of Jesus Christ and everything that went with it; they were baptised 'in the name of Jesus'. They began to share the experience which made them worship God as Three-in-One; they were baptised 'in the name of the Father and the Son and the Holy Spirit'. They joined a new people under Jesus as Lord, a people which refused to admit that any class distinctions, or barriers of any kind, had any right to spoil its fellowship. That is why Matthew's gospel ends with a picture of Jesus saying to his 'disciples' (which means pupils): 'Go forth and make all nations my disciples; baptise men everywhere . . .'

In the early Christian centuries, the meaning of baptism was based on the conversion of an adult. A man or a woman accepted Jesus as Lord and Saviour, and accepted the key points of the Church's teaching. Then he or she was immersed in the water – and it felt like death, like the death of all the evil past, like Christ's own death which offered hope for the future. Then he or she arose from the water, and what had seemed like burial now seemed like birth. As Paul reminded the Christians in Corinth, in his second letter: 'When anyone is united to Christ, there is a new world; the old order has gone, and a new order has already begun' (5.17).

That is still the meaning of baptism for adults who become Christians, as millions have over the last hundred years. Any parish priest or chaplin is always delighted to welcome candidates for adult baptism. But since about AD 200 (probably since the time described in the New Testament – but the evidence is not certain), babies born in Christian families have been baptised. The Christians who are called 'Baptists' disagree with this policy, but Anglicans, like most Christians, accept it.

The baptism of children who cannot make statements or decisions for themselves is right when there is a reasonable likelihood that they will be brought up as Christians. In homes where the parents cannot honestly promise to encourage their children to accept Jesus Christ as their Lord, baptism would be a mockery. It will help towards greater honesty to use in such cases a service which expresses God's love and blessing but which does not include baptism.

In the baptism of children of Christian parents, faith is present – the faith of the parents and of the specially appointed Christian friends known as 'godparents'. But because the infant being baptised is helpless, this service brings out dramatically the truth that in the whole story of God's people God's reality matters even more than man's response. Before we can do anything at all, God's people is there first. God's people invites us to enter its life, which flourished long before we were born and will continue long after our deaths. And at the head of God's people is the living Christ, blessing the children and calling the diciples as he did in Palestine. And behind the call of Jesus is the initiative of God, who creates and rules and who in his great love chooses us to be his people. Any Christian can administer baptism; in an emergency, it is not necessary to find a priest first. What matters is the new birth and the new welcome into the new family: the Church.

Whether we receive it as children or as adults, baptism makes us members of God's people. We are now (so to speak) recruits in Christ's army and limbs of Christ's body. What, then, is Confirmation?

In the life of the Church of England, the service of Confirmation is the time when those who have already been baptised declare their acceptance of the Christian faith and life. They do so in front of the bishop, and then they are admitted by him into the full privileges of membership. 'Confirmation' comes from the Latin for 'Strengthening', and in this service the bishop prays that these Christians may be strengthened with the gifts of the Holy Spirit, as promised to God's people. Then the bishop – representing the whole Church, the Church in every time and place – lays his hands on each candidate. It is the ancient sign of blessing, often repeated in the Bible, particularly in *The Acts of the Apostles* when St Peter and St John pray that some Samaritans who have been baptised may 'receive the Holy Spirit' (8.14–17).

Any parish priest is glad to prepare a candidate for Confirmation. The Church has no rule about the right age. The best guidance is that a boy or girl ought to seek Confirmation as soon as he or she has real, personal understanding of what it means to belong to the Christian group – to the Body of Christ. You need not understand much! Even the greatest Christians have understood only a little.

I I

We inherit history

SOME FAMILIES have kept letters written by members of those families a century or more ago. One of these letters may describe hearing the news of Nelson's victory at Trafalgar – or the news of the execution of Charles I. Letters of this sort make English history come vividly alive. And it is entirely proper for you to think of *the Bible* as a collection of letters and other documents belonging to your family, for if you are a member of the Church you belong to the family that wrote the Bible.

You are cheating yourself if you don't make yourself at home in the Bible, and if you deny yourself the instruction and encouragement which it alone can give. Regular study of the Bible is a very important way in which the whole Church listens to God, and it is best if you can manage your own reading of the Bible every day with the help of the notes provided by the Bible Reading Fellowship or the Scripture Union. But since you live in a world which is very different from the world when the Bible was written, you naturally ask: what authority does the Bible have over you?

It cannot be the authority of a book that is always right. For one thing, it is not a single book but a whole library of books, and the books are very different in their purpose and their value. For another thing, the Bible contains different accounts of the same events, beginning with the difference between the accounts of the creation of the world in the first two chapters of Genesis. One opinion in the Bible may be contradicted by another – for example, the New Testament often contradicts the Old. When trying to reconstruct the history which lies behind the accounts given in the Bible, it is essential to use the results of modern scholarly investigations. When trying to think out what it means for your life today, it is essential to use your intelligence. What is called 'Fundamentalism' – that is, the belief that the Bible contains no errors, a belief regarded by some as fundamental to Christianity – is wrong.

The authority of the Bible is the weight of the experience of the people who wrote it, and of the people about whom they wrote. For they experienced the activity of God in events which changed the course of history. They had the insight to see what those events meant, and they had the skill to write about it.

About 2,000 years before Christ's birth, Abraham left his home and the rich life he had known by the river Euphrates, and in his wanderings through Palestine and the surrounding desert he experienced God in a new way. The God of Abraham became the God of his son Isaac and his grandson Jacob. And to this day, he is the God of Jews and Christians.

Hundreds of years later the descendants of Abraham were in Egypt, but they left that rich civilisation by the river Nile and began their wanderings again – this time under Moses. The religion they formed in that new period in the desert, before they entered Palestine, inspired much of the Old Testament and still has great influence today – for example, through the Ten Commandments.

The commandments show that this religion was meant to be as clean as the desert itself. God's people were to worship him alone – not worshipping also the gods which represented sex, power and good harvests; not bowing down to gods which were no more than carved statues; not using God's name lightly. Every seven days, a whole day was to be set aside for rest and worship. And God's people were to treat each other with dignity. Fathers and mothers were to be honoured. There was to be no murder or theft. There were to be no false accusations. Each man's wife, family and property were to be respected as his, within the fellowship of God's people.

When Jesus came, he summed up the commandments in two – both quoted from other parts of the Old Testament. God must be loved with the whole personality. One's neighbours must be loved as one loves oneself. And by 'neighbour' Jesus meant every other human being. In other words, treat them as you want to be treated yourself! God's people must never be exclusive! But before that understanding of God's people could be reached, much had to happen. For one thing, the Jewish nation had to lose its political independence.

About a thousand years before Christ, Saul the first King of the Jews was replaced by the more attractive and successful David – and David was succeeded by his son Solomon. It was David who made Jerusalem the capital. It was Solomon who built the temple in Jerusalem. But the ideal of wise government and glorious worship did not last. First the Northern Kingdom of the Jews, around Samaria, fell to the Assyrian invaders (721 BC). Then Jerusalem fell to the empire of Babylon (597 BC). However, during the quarrels, corruptions and tragedies of these years a highly impressive line of men, the prophets, arose. Amos, one of the first of the great prophets, was a shepherd demanding justice in society rather than sacrifices in the temple. Jeremiah preached with a rare courage against the nationalism of his own people in Jerusalem.

When some of the Jews were allowed to return to Jerusalem, their return was celebrated in the sublime poetry which we can read in chapters 40-55 of the Book of Isaiah. Although disappointments and disasters followed their return to Jerusalem, and some of the Jews naturally grew narrow and bitter, this amazing people never completely forgot the pure religion of the Ten Commandments and the prophets.

It was in this period that the Old Testament was put together. 'Testament' means 'covenant' or 'agreement'. The Old Testament expressed the faith that God had made an agreement with Abraham and his descendants, for ever. The Ten Commandments and the other laws associated with Moses attempted to state what God demanded, as his side of the bargain, and the prophets frequently denounced Israel for failing to live up to the agreement. But God was patient and loyal, and Jeremiah (for one) looked forward to 'a new covenant ... This is the covenant ... says the Lord, I will set my law within them and write it on their hearts; I will become their God and they shall become my people' (31.31–33).

Basically, that is the promise with which the Old Testament ends. The promise does not come true in the events covered by the Old Testament. Nor does the answer come in the books called the *Apocrypha*, which in many Bibles are printed between the Old and the New Testaments. These are books of varying value. They formed part of the Old Testament in Greek for the Jews who are now scattered in many places, but were not acknowledged by the Jews in Palestine as having the same authority as the main books of the law, the prophets and the histories.

But the answer came. A new covenant between God and man was made. God's people moved forward into a new age.

The life of Jesus cannot be understood unless you remember that the Old Testament was what he was taught in the school at Nazareth, and the Old Testament was what he could quote – to himself when asking himself in the desert what his work was going to be, and to others when his work became the preaching (by word and deed) of the good news of God's rule. For example, Jesus referred to himself as the 'Son of Man', an expression then commonly used. To understand the reference, you have to turn to the seventh chapter of the Book of Daniel, where there is a dream of the 'Son of Man' going in glory to God. There, the 'Son of Man' is a man who represents God's people.

Jesus never wrote a book. He lived a life, and he founded a new community, God's new people, growing from the first twelve. But some of the letters written by St Paul have survived, to give us authentic and unforgettable pictures of the living faith of the Church in its early years. So have a few other documents – for example, St John the Divine's vision of the complete triumph of Jesus, written in the Roman concentration camp on the island of Patmos: 'Then I saw a new heaven and a new earth. . . . I saw the holy city, new Jerusalem, coming down out of heaven from God, made ready like a bride adorned for her husband' (21.1, 2). And four gospels have been treasured by the Christians from the first century AD onwards. 'Gospel' means 'good news'.

The oldest and shortest of these gospels is by St Mark, a personal assistant both to St Paul and St Peter. He probably wrote it in Rome soon after the execution of those two great leaders, to strengthen his fellow-Christians for martyrdom (a word which means 'witness', for these Christians regarded their deaths as acts of witness to the living Christ). Matthew's gospel presents Jesus as the new Moses, and includes the Sermon on the Mount. St Luke (a doctor) portrays Jesus as the healer and friend, and gives us most of the famous parables; and this gospel is followed by a second volume, *The Acts of the Apostles*, showing how the message and work of Jesus spread from Jerusalem to Rome. John's gospel goes deeper than the others and is the fruit of long experience. It shows what the coming of Jesus means, as the light of the world.

Gradually the Christians agreed that the four gospels, with Paul's letters and some other documents, were so valuable that they must be put alongside the Old Testament, as the Christian 'scriptures' (or writings). When the Roman empire did its utmost to stamp out Christianity, the persecutors tried to get hold of the scriptures and destroy them. Those Christians who handed the books over were called the *traditores*; from the word comes our 'traitors'.

God's people existed before these books were written. The stories of Abraham, Moses and the Kings of Israel were told around camp fires before they were told in books. The story of Jesus was told in Christian sermons before it was told in the gospels. But these books, when written, were rightly honoured, because with a tremendous power they told of the events which had created God's people. Their authority for God's people was now unique. And although many hundreds of thousands of books have been written in the course of time, discussing the significance of the events recorded in the Bible, no book has ever been given the authority which the Bible will now always have.

Preaching to the Athenians and writing to the Romans, Paul taught that God had to a certain extent revealed himself to people who were neither Jews nor Christians. In our time, when it is easier than ever before for Christians to understand and appreciate other religious traditions, there is more agreement than ever to respect much that is good and true in the scriptures of the Muslims, Hindus, Buddhists and others. There is only one God, and it is clear that he is called by many names and worshipped according to many traditions. But it remains true that nowhere in the history of the world have there been events with results similar to the results of the events recorded in the Bible; and nowhere in the literature of the world is there a library like the Christians' Bible.

Millions of people remain loyal Jews despite many persecutions, the worst of which were inflicted by people calling themselves Christians. Inevitably these Jews do not place the books of the New Testament on the same level as those of the Old – although many Jews are prepared to recognise Jesus as a great Jewish prophet and to forgive Christians for their cruelties. It is right for Christians to admit that they have lost much by getting out of touch with Jews, and that they have often behaved towards Jews in a way which is plainly condemned by Jesus. But it is also right for Christians to make their great claims about Jesus. For Jesus summed up all that was best in the Old Testament, while getting rid of the national pride and the insistence on strict obedience to detailed religious laws. Jesus showed that all men and women, including the strictest Jews, were sinners – and Jesus offered all a new start. It was in truth a new convenant, written on the hearts of all who responded to the challenge and appeal of Jesus.

As the centuries passed, the number of Christians grew into millions. Amazingly, the Christian Church proved stronger than the Roman Empire which tried to suppress it. The more it was made to suffer, the stronger the Church grew; the blood of martyrs was the seed of the Church.

From one not very important part of the Roman Empire, Judea, the Christian faith was carried as far as another, Britain – where the first and most famous martyr was Alban, put to death in 305 (or thereabouts). Within three hundred years of the death of Jesus, a Christian (Constantine) was Emperor of Rome. When the Empire was overwhelmed by the surrounding barbarians, the Church remained standing – the guardian not only of the Christian faith but also of civilisation, knowledge, gentleness, law and order. Only in some provinces such as Britain did the Church disappear with the Empire. And the work of the Christian missionaries survived and flourished in Cornwall, Wales, Ireland and the lowlands of Scotland, inspired by saints such as David (in Wales), Patrick (in Ireland), Ninian and Columba (in Scotland).

It was because the Church played such a vitally important role in European history after the fall of the Roman Empire that it became so powerful – so deeply respected, and so wealthy. In Rome the Popes became world-leaders, much as the Emperors had been. The first great Pope, Gregory, saw it as his mission not only to centralise authority in his own hands but also to conquer new lands for Christianity. With great boldness Gregory sent Augustine from Rome to England in 597, as the first Archbishop of Canterbury; and Ethelbert, King of Kent, was soon converted.

Slowly England became part of the Catholic Church. In the North the most heroic missionaries – men such as St Cuthbert who lies buried in Durham Cathedral, or St Chad the first Bishop of Lichfield – looked for inspiration not to Canterbury but to the holy islands of Iona (off Scotland) and Lindisfarne (off Northumberland). But gradually all the English Christians were brought together into one Church under the Pope and the Archbishops of Canterbury and York. In fact the English Church was one while the country was still divided into tribal kingdoms. It became famous for its scholars such as Bede in Jarrow, and for its Christian kings such as Alfred the Great, King of Wessex, and Edward the Confessor, who founded Westminster Abbey. In its turn England produced missionaries such as Boniface, the man from Devon who led the chief Christian mission in Germany.

The Norman conquest of England in 1066 linked England more firmly with the rest of Europe, and the Norman churches which still survive are reminders of the strength and discipline brought by the invaders. But the Church became in many ways a champion of freedom. Archbishop Anselm, a famous philosopher, stood up to William the Conqueror's son. Thomas Becket resisted Henry II and was murdered by Henry's knights in Canterbury Cathedral (1170). Another Archbishop of Canterbury, Stephen Langton, was at the head of the barons who forced King John to accept the English liberties set forth in Magna Carta (1215).

More important than politics was the growth in mind and spirit in the Middle Ages. Schools, universities and hospitals were founded. The monks, giving themselves to the worship of God, were in many cases also good farmers or scholars. The friars – monks not confined to a monastery – took the love of Christ to the poor of the towns, following the examples of St Francis in Italy and St Dominic in France. Some saintly bishops such as Hugh of Lincoln inspired the parishes. On pilgrimage to the tomb of Thomas Becket, a pageant of humanity in the fourteenth century passes through the pages of Geoffrey Chaucer's *Canterbury Tales*, and noble writings have been left by more spiritually minded Christians such as Lady Julian of Norwich. Some purity was lost when the Church became so closely identified with a whole society. (For example, the Church now permitted 'just' wars although the early Christians had been pacifists, rejecting everything to do with war.) But there were many gains.

The Christian civilisation of the Middle Ages was broken up by many changes in the sixteenth century, the age of Reformation. Today it seems a vanished world. But you can feel its beauty and its faith near you if you go into an old cathedral or parish church, or if you listen to an old carol or to the sound of church bells. You can then realise for yourself that some rich and astonishing chapters in the story of God's people were written when the Bible had been completed. All this is today your heritage.

12

We are Anglicans

THE CHRISTIAN CHURCH is tragically divided. It ought to be possible just to say, 'We are Christians'. But the fact is that in order to be a full Christian you have to gather regularly with your fellow-Christians, and in order to do this you have to belong to one of the Churches into which the Christian Church is now split.

The 'Ecumenical' (from the Greek for 'world-wide') movement for Christian unity has developed since about 1910, and has already made great advances. The relationships between the divided Churches have been transformed. In many practical ways they co-operate, and over more and more theological problems they agree. There is no good reason why our present divisions should continue for much longer. On the contrary, it is widely agreed that the need is great for reunion between the Churches – a union of the kind that Christ commands, but the way he wishes us to follow. What is that way? This urgent question cannot be answered unless we pray for guidance, and unless we take trouble to meet members of other Churches. If we are to unite with each other, we must love each other; and if we are to love each other, we must meet.

Anglicans are proud to belong to the World Council of Churches, formed in 1948, and to national councils such as the British Council of Churches, formed in 1942. Almost all Anglican congregations take part in the life and work of the local Council of Churches. During the

1960s and 1970s many links of understanding and friendship have been formed with the Roman Catholic Church, and there have been negotiations for full reunion with Methodists, Presbyterians and others. (Methodism was founded by an Anglican, John Wesley, who died in 1791. Presbyterians believe that the 'presbyter' should be the senior officer in the Church, and do not have bishops.) Anglicans already belong to some United Churches overseas – but not yet in Britain.

Anglicans have no right to condemn any other Church. Instead, they gladly acknowledge that God has blessed and used their fellow-Christians in many ways. All that Anglicans need to say is that while the Christian Churches still pray and work for reunion it is right for Anglicans to be proud of their heritage. The Anglican tradition preserves the essential beliefs which are held in common by all Christians. It also contains many treasures which are its own but which should be contributed to the wider Church in the fuller unity which must come.

The word 'Anglican' comes from 'English', because the pattern of life in the modern, world-wide Anglican Communion was set by the changes made in the Church of England during the Reformation of the sixteenth century. These were great changes, made possible by the rejection of the claims of the Popes at the time.

The Bible and the church services were translated from Latin into English so that all could understand. Christian faith and Christian life became simpler and were freed from control by the priests. But the churches inherited from the Middle Ages were still used, and there was much continuity in what went on inside them. The Church of England emerged from the Reformation both Protestant and Catholic in spirit, although its conservatism was criticised by many other Protestants and its refusal to obey the Pope was regarded as heretical by many other Catholics.

Some of the reasons for these changes were political.

Henry VIII sought from the Pope an end to his marriage with Catherine of Aragon. And in Rome the Pope refused. The King's reply was that no foreigner such as the Pope must be allowed any authority in England. Between 1532 and 1534 seven Acts of Parliament separated the Church of England from Rome – and made the King himself its 'supreme head' on earth. But it was not simply a question of a lustful (and repulsive) monarch wanting a divorce. Actually, what he wanted was a decree of 'nullity' to say that his marriage with Catherine had been no marriage at all, for she had first been the wife of his dead brother Arthur – and, quoting the book *Leviticus* in the Bible which prohibited marriage with a dead brother's wife, Henry persuaded himself that Catherine's failure to produce a son was a sign of God's wrath. What really mattered was that Henry needed a son and heir; it was dangerous to leave the crown of England to a woman.

Curiously, it was under a queen, Elizabeth I, that the Church of England achieved a settlement which proved lasting apart from some twenty years in the middle of the seventeenth century. In 1649 Oliver Cromwell and other extreme Protestants or 'Puritans' succeeded in overthrowing and executing Charles I, one of the charges against the King being his loyalty to the Anglican way of running the Church. But the Puritan revolution was not permanent. The Church of England was established once more as the National Church in 1660, and when James II, who had been converted to Roman Catholicism, tried to alter this, it was the King who found himself in exile (in 1688). The Church of England prevailed against Oliver Cromwell and James II because this National Church had firmly taken root in the English soil. It had been 'established' by the State, but more important: it was loved by many of the people.

When England became the centre of a vast empire over the next 250 years, naturally Englishmen took the customs of their National Church wherever they went. So

Anglicanism was built up in the United States and Canada, in India and Africa, in Australia and New Zealand, and in many other places around the world.

But to say that the Church of England's history cannot be separated from the history of England, or that the missionary expansion of Anglicanism accompanied the expansion of the British Empire, merely tells us something about the past. It does not answer the question whether Anglicanism has the right to survive now when England is different. Nor does it answer the question whether anyone outside England is right to remain an Anglican now that English domination has been rejected. There are, for example, flourishing Anglican Churches in Scotland, Wales and Ireland. The Anglican or 'Protestant Episcopal' Church in the United States is important not only to its own great nation but also to the whole of Anglicanism. The Anglican Churches in Africa are growing fast. Of all the Anglicans confirmed in 1973, less than a quarter were English. What sense does this make?

It is right to answer that the Church of England and other Churches in the world-wide Anglican Communion have shown – as the great Orthodox Churches of Russia, Greece and other countries have also shown – that it is possible to remain full members of the Catholic Church without acknowledging the modern claims of the Popes.

This is important because under the modern Popes the Roman Catholic Church has made what others regard as mistakes. The worst mistake was to lay down that the Pope is infallible! On page 62 we saw what this means in Roman Catholic belief; here, we have room only to add that infallibility seems to be claimed for two doctrines about the mother of Jesus – doctrines not found in the New Testament. The first, defined in 1854, teaches that the Blessed Virgin Mary was from her conception free from all stain of basic or 'original' sin; this is the doctrine of the 'immaculate conception'. The second, defined in

1950, teaches that, having completed her earthly life, she was carried into heaven in her body as well as in her soul; this is the doctrine of the 'assumption'. Other teachings by the modern Popes are not usually claimed to be infallible but have been presented as teachings which all Roman Catholics must accept – for example, the teaching that it is wrong to control births by using artificial means of contraception. Almost all Anglicans disagree with the Pope on these points – and are glad that, despite this, they can still be Catholics.

But that is being negative! To be positive, we can rightly claim that Anglicanism has proved its spiritual value (although it has been far from perfect). That can be shown by the great poets to whom the Church of England has been a home – among them William Shakespeare, John Donne, George Herbert, William Cowper, William Wordsworth, S. T. Coleridge, John Keble, Alfred Tennyson, Matthew Arnold, Christina Rossetti, T. S. Eliot, W. H. Auden. Such poets would not have loved the Church of England if it was nothing more than the cold institution described by its critics. They have found something alive, authentic and good in the life of their English Church – its beautiful services, its constant emphasis on the Bible, its tolerance, its respect for the views and interests of laymen, its rich variety, its dignity and stability.

Anglican worship has been 'corporate' or 'common' (all together) but dignified. Thomas Cranmer, then Archbishop of Canterbury, edited the Book of Common Prayer – one of the noblest books in the English language, able to speak to the heart but almost all the time maintaining the highest standards of beauty. It was issued in 1549, but changes were made in 1552, 1559, 1604 and 1662. Another very influential Anglican prayer book was issued for Scotland in 1637. This was unpopular among most of the Scots, but something unexpected happened later. When the United States had won their independence, it was in Scotland

97

that the first Anglican bishop for America was consecrated (1784) – and so this Scottish prayer book influenced the first American prayer book (1789).

In recent years almost all the Anglican Churches in the world have issued more modern services, since the language of 1549 or 1637 is no longer always understood. Many of these services have allowed greater freedom than Cranmer thought proper, so that contemporary concerns and hopes can be voiced. Another great enrichment has come through the increasing use of hymns – some of them now old and very famous, but some new and experimental. There has also been the development of music for the choir and the organ. A great musical tradition has grown up since the Book of Common Prayer was first printed, and every century including our own has added to it. The music in some Anglican cathedrals and college chapels is world-renowned, and the Royal School of Church Music unites many thousands of parish church choirs in aiming at the best. But across the centuries the backbone of Anglican worship has remained essentially unchanged. It is the use of words known to all, as a way of offering the prayer of all.

This worship is dominated by the Bible. For hundreds of years churchgoers loved to hear the magnificent English of the psalms (the Old Testament's hymns) as translated by Bishop Miles Coverdale in 1535 – and the lessons from the Authorised Version of the Bible issued in 1611, during Shakespeare's lifetime. Then modern translations became necessary. The most official in recent years is the New English Bible, completed in 1970 under the sponsorship of many Churches. These modern translations are being used in more and more churches. Still, however, the principle remains: our common prayer is best when together we have heard the Word of God through the 'Scriptures', the writings gathered in the Bible. Anglicans sit under the Bible.

Anglican 'doctrine' or teaching is therefore based on

98

the Bible. This is the Church of England's official definition, adopted in 1973: 'The doctrine of the Church of England is grounded in the holy Scriptures, and in such teachings of the ancient Fathers and Councils of the Church as are agreeable to the said Scriptures. In particular such doctrine is found in the Thirty-nine Articles of Religion, the Book of Common Prayer, and the Ordinal.' The 'Articles of Religion' mentioned in that definition are a document, last revised in 1572, stating the Church of England's position in the theological controversies of the time. The Ordinal is the collection of services for 'ordaining' or setting aside the clergy.

This does *not* mean that Anglican life is confined to what was laid down explicitly in the Bible or in the ancient Church or in the Tudor age. No! Anglicanism has been a living experience, changing as faithful Christians have changed. Successive generations, and very different groups and individuals, have added to the riches of Anglican worship and to the vigour of Anglican life.

In Anglicanism, lay people matter. Almost all the clergy have spent a lot of their time among laymen, visiting people in their homes and trying to help people with problems. Many priests have served as chaplains in schools and colleges, in the Forces, in industry, in hospitals, holiday camps and prisons. The Anglican conviction is that the Church ought to be thoroughly involved in the life of the nation.

In the Church of England, all who live in the area known as the 'parish' are regarded as this Church's responsibility unless they belong to another religious body; the parish church is their church. All who worship regularly in that church, and who are baptised and over seventeen, are entitled to have their names on the 'electoral roll'. Each year those on this list elect the Parochial Church Council, which co-operates with the rector or vicar in the initiation, conduct and development of church work both within the parish and outside – and which controls most of the parish church's financial and other affairs. The chief lay officers are the two church-wardens, elected annually and assisted by elected 'sides-men'.

At any rate since the eighteenth century, Anglican laymen have been encouraged to think for themselves, and have been free to do so without fear of heresy-hunts. Priests have also been encouraged to be scholars and thinkers, with the freedom needed to seek truth and express it. For example, Anglicanism has encouraged the study of the Bible by scientifically historical methods, specially in the great English universities of Oxford, Cambridge, London and Durham. The teachers of the Church have been men (and some women) educated alongside laymen, familiar with contemporary thought, and often teaching and writing in the universities. And the Church has been heavily involved in education at almost every level. For centuries, the Church of England controlled almost all the schools in the nation. Still this Church maintains many thousands of church schools, and also colleges of education for training teachers, within the national system. A typically Anglican prayer is that 'true religion and sound learning' may flourish together.

This involvement in the life of society has brought great problems. For example, there has been the problem of the relationship of *religion and politics*.

For centuries the Church of England has been controlled by the English Crown and Parliament, representing the lay people of England. Now that the Church has its own democratic assemblies (the Church of England has its General Synod, and also Diocesan and Deanery Synods) most people feel that these are the bodies that ought to speak up on behalf of the layman. So the links between Church and State in England are being altered. No other Anglican Church has recently been controlled by the government of its country. Anglicanism in Ireland ceased to be 'established' by the State in 1871; in Wales, in 1920.

The problem of religion and politics has led to many controversies. Most members of the Church are nervous about 'mixing religion and politics', and are particularly suspicious of priests who 'get mixed up in politics'. This is understandable. Christianity has a message which goes far deeper than any political programme could ever do, and the Church should not be identified with any political party. But there ought to be some connection between religion and politics. Religion ought to inspire us with the vision of God's love for men. Politics ought to drive us into loving action to help those in need – according to our own consciences, not according to any clergyman's dictation. Christians ought therefore to express their love by active service, whether they do this by taking a political role or by quietly trying to help those around them.

Some famous Anglican thinkers have disturbed the complacent by preaching a vision of a society founded on brotherhood and justice. The greatest names in the past (in England) are those of the Victorian, F. D. Maurice, and the two twentieth-century bishops, Charles Gore (of Birmingham and Oxford) and William Temple (of Manchester, York and Canterbury). Some Anglicans have taken the lead in protests against injustices and evil. In nineteenth-century England, for example, William Wilberforce campaigned against the trade in slaves, Josephine Butler against the men who made money out of prostitutes, and Lord Shaftesbury against the use of children as labourers in factories and mines.

The best way of honouring that great Anglican tradition is to carry on the battle for a better society in our own day. Not all Anglicans are heroic enough, but at least they do know where the Church stands and where their duty lies on many issues. For example, the Church is in the thick of the fight against racial prejudice and the colour bar. The Anglican leadership in this fight in South

Africa has been brave and has won world-wide respect. The same fight goes on in Britain.

In many parishes a 'Street Warden' scheme is in operation. That means that every street in the area is served by a churchgoer who tries to welcome newcomers, to keep in touch with the old and lonely, and to help wherever there is an emergency such as illness. The Street Warden is a friend – an informal and voluntary ally of the State's medical and social services. Many other examples of Christian action could be given. For every member of the Church needs to *do* what the parable of the good Samaritan teaches – being a neighbour means being a friend to every person in need.

Problems of a very different sort have been raised by the work of the scholars on the Bible and on the traditions of the Church. Anglican scholars, possessing so much freedom, have often reached critical conclusions. These have often challenged the orthodoxy of less critical members of the Church. Such problems have led to fierce controversies, but in these – as in debates on political matters – the view of the Church as a whole has not been finally expressed by any bishop or other leader. The mind of the Church has been made known gradually, as a result of free thought and free speech.

It is sometimes suggested that Anglicanism is a mere debating society, composed of individuals who are so 'liberal' that they agree about nothing. But Anglicanism has in it strong Evangelical and strong Catholic elements, reminding it that it exists in order to be obedient to Jesus Christ.

The *Evangelical* (or 'Low Church') movement in Anglicanism safeguards the insistence of the Protestant Reformation on the right and the duty of each person to make his or her own decision to be reconciled to God through Jesus Christ. There is great emphasis on the fact that salvation from sin is the free gift of God, not earned by any good that man may do but given to those who in simple trust accept Jesus Christ as Saviour and Lord. With this goes a great emphasis on the privilege and duty of personal Bible study. Worship is simple, making clear that what matters is the response to the message in the Bible. And resulting from this, there is great emphasis on evangelism – spreading the good news of Jesus Christ.

Anglican Evangelicals have been suspected of sentimentality but they have often been marked by enthusiasm and attractiveness in daily life, for their Bible-based religion has been warmly personal. Evangelicalism revived during the eighteenth century – at a time when much of the rest of Anglican life had grown cold because of a dull emphasis on being moderate, reasonable and respectable. In the twentieth century, Evangelicalism is reviving again – and again it is meeting a spiritual need.

The *Catholic* (or 'High Church') movement in Anglicanism safeguards the continuity with the Church before the Reformation, while not accepting the claims of the Popes or many customs which are regarded as corruptions of the early form of Catholicism.

Anglo-Catholicism tends to have more elaborate services, and to stress the traditions of the Church. It was strong during the seventeenth century as a reaction against the Puritanism of Oliver Cromwell and the like. It revived during the nineteenth century, in what was known as the Oxford Movement, as a reaction against compromise with the materialism of modern society. It has restored much of the old beauty to churches and church services – and has restored the old insistence on personal holiness through self-discipline. The Anglican communities of monks and nuns have been examples to many.

Anglo-Catholicism has often been suspected as an attempt to take people back to the religion of the Middle Ages. But whatever may be our opinions about details, the Catholic movement in Anglicanism is surely right to remind us that Anglicanism is not a separate religion. On the contrary, Anglicanism is loyal to what the great majority of Christians have believed and done in the Catholic Church since the beginning.

Anglicanism accepts and devoutly uses the two *sacraments* founded by Jesus Christ himself. These are Baptism and Holy Communion. A sacrament has been described (in the Church of England's Revised Catechism, 1962), as 'the use of material things as signs and pledges of God's grace, and as a means by which we receive his gifts'. For example, the use of water in Baptism is a sign of God's saving goodness, and a means of receiving it.

Anglicanism also accepts and devoutly repeats the two *creeds* which have come down from the days before the Church was divided.

One is called the 'Apostles' Creed'. It was not written by the apostles, but it began in the teaching given to candidates for Baptism in Rome and elsewhere. The word 'apostle' means 'envoy', and this creed states briefly – almost as in a telegram – what was thought to be essential in the message which the apostles passed on to the Church. The other creed is called the 'Nicene Creed', from the Council of the Church held in 325 in the town of Nicaea. (Some words were added later.) It states briefly what was thought to be most important in the Church's faith that Jesus was both truly human and truly divine. Another, longer document called the 'Athanasian Creed' is also printed in many prayer books, although nowadays it is seldom used. But the majestic hymn 'We praise thee, O God' (in Latin, *Te Deum laudamus*), written in about 400, is often sung or said in Anglican worship.

Essentially, what Anglicans do when they use these creeds, or sing *Te Deum*, is to state that they are glad to stand in the tradition of faith which the creeds have expressed for so long. They are the heirs of the ages, proud to belong to the brotherhood of the baptised.

Anglicanism also accepts and honours the threefold *ministry* of bishops, priests and deacons. The system of having bishops as leaders is known as 'episcopacy'. Bishops have been the main leaders of the Church since the second century, and in many ways they carry on the work of the apostles. A bishop is a 'father-in-God' to the clergy and the people in his area, his 'diocese'. He is also a teacher of the Christian and Catholic faith, and a planner and inspirer of evangelism and further advance. 'Priest' is the shortened form of the word 'presbyter', or elder. Priests preside at the Holy Communion, lead local congregations, try to reach all who need their help, and assure sinners of God's forgiveness and healing. 'Deacon' is from a Greek word meaning 'servant' (and 'ministry' is from a Latin word meaning 'service'). In Anglicanism, the man who is a deacon is usually in training to be a priest. But the Church is also served and led by a considerable number of women known as deaconesses.

Each Anglican diocese is grouped with others in a 'province'. In the British Isles, for example, there are the provinces of Canterbury and York, and other provinces known as the Church in Wales, the Church in Ireland and the Episcopal Church in Scotland (which, because it still wanted to be led by bishops, split from the National Church, the Church of Scotland, when that Church finally became Presbyterian in 1690).

Each Anglican province manages its own affairs and has its own character. But each is in 'communion' or full fellowship with the Church of England and in particular with the Archbishop of Canterbury, who is the 'Primate' or senior bishop of 'All England'. Once every ten years all the Anglican bishops meet in the Lambeth Conference. It is so called from Lambeth Palace, the London home of the Archbishops of Canterbury since the twelfth century. Every other year, the smaller Anglican Consultative Council meets, wherever it chooses.

The threefold ministry of bishop, priest and deacon is

based on the Catholic way of ordaining them – by prayer with the 'laying on of hands' by a bishop. At the consecration of a new bishop, a minimum of three other bishops must 'lay on hands' in prayer. There is no evidence that in the first centuries of Christianity the Popes of Rome were treated as they came to be treated in the Middle Ages – and as they have been treated by modern Roman Catholics. But there is plenty of evidence that from those early times the work of Catholic bishops, priests and deacons has been of great importance. And although the Reformation in the sixteenth century caused many controversies about the nature of the ordained ministry, there is plenty of evidence that those controversies are dying down nowadays. In recent years, representatives of Anglicanism have held careful talks with Roman Catholics, with Presbyterians and with Methodists – and have joined them in publishing documents to show how much the Churches agree.

The work of bishops, priests and deacons has been work for Christ, representing Christ. It has been part of the vitality of the Catholic Church – which since the sixteenth century has (Anglicans believe) included Anglicanism.

13

We take part in the Holy Communion

EVERY FULL member of the Church ought to take part regularly in the Holy Communion if he or she can.

People sometimes ask: why go to church, when you can watch hymn-singing and discussions on TV? There are two answers. The first is that some people are in rebellion against the tyranny of TV. When they want to worship God, as they regularly do, they want to do it themselves in company with their fellow-Christians, and not leave it to the few who appear on the TV screen. When they want to hear the good news from God expounded and interpreted, they prefer listening to a preacher who is human in front of them (despite all his imperfections), to listening to a discussion in a TV studio. They enjoy the beauty and peace of the building. They enjoy singing with people they know. They enjoy meeting friends after-wards – and they may even enjoy the walk!

Perhaps that first reason for going to church may not convince you. Knowing how good some of the religious programmes are, you may prefer to stay at home watching. But there is a second reason for going to church, and it is a far stronger one. *No TV set has been invented which passes bread and wine round, making a Christian community.*

This is the one service which Jesus Christ himself founded – at his last supper with the twelve apostles. It has been the heart of Christian worship ever since that evening in the upper room in Jerusalem – in the age of TV just as in the days when almost all Christians lived close to the land they cultivated; in an English city just as in a Roman catacomb where the Christians took refuge from persecution underground. Through many centuries already, this has been the mystery which has gathered the followers of Jesus and kept them close to him in the life he came to bring – life abundant and eternal.

Paul's first letter to the Christians in Corinth contains the earliest surviving description of the Holy Communion, in chapter 11.

'The tradition which I handed on to you came to me from the Lord himself: that the Lord Jesus, on the night of his arrest, took bread and, after giving thanks to God, broke it and said: "This is my body, which is for you; do this as a memorial of me." In the same way, he took the cup after supper and said: "This cup is the new covenant sealed by my blood. Whenever you drink it, do this as a memorial of me." For every time you eat this bread and drink the cup, you proclaim the death of the Lord, until he comes.'

At that last supper before his arrest, Jesus gave thanks over the bread and wine. It was the Jewish way of saying 'grace' at a meal. When the first Christians repeated this action, it was during the course of a meal together – as Paul's letter shows. Before long the Holy Communion was made a separate service (in order to avoid problems to which Paul's letter refers), although often in our time those who have taken part in it do gather immediately afterwards for a meal or at least for a cup of coffee or tea. Here at once we see part of the meaning of this act. It is an act done by people with glad and grateful hearts. It is an act in which they enjoy some of the good things in God's creation as they eat and drink. And it is an act of fellowship.

For Christians, this is the family party. Its joy and its

togetherness were indicated by Paul in the same letter. 'When we bless "the cup of blessing", is it not a means of sharing in the blood of Christ? When we break the bread, is it not a means of sharing in the body of Christ? Because there is one loaf, we, many as we are, are one body; for it is one loaf of which we all partake.' In other words, this eating and this drinking make Christians remember what they are – the Body of Christ!

It is a special kind of eating and drinking, for it is done in remembrance of Jesus. Just as the bread and the wine are taken to the 'altar' or holy table, and are taken by the priest who presides, so the life of Jesus was taken to disclose the life of God. Just as the bread is broken in order to be eaten, so the body of Jesus was broken on the cross in order to be used as the instrument of our liberation, as the placard of God's love. Just as the wine is poured out, so the blood of Jesus was shed in that great battle against evil. It is a memorial – a grateful, proud and triumphant proclamation! But it is more. When Christians eat this and drink this, they do *not* remember an absent friend who died long ago. They 'do this' in the conviction that their Lord is alive – and is present among them.

Through this sacrament, he is among his followers today with as much power as when he sat or stood among the apostles at the beginning. (If you are troubled by the fact that many people seem little influenced by the Holy Communion, remember how often those who saw Jesus physically failed to understand him.) Of course the bread is not his body, or the wine his blood, physically. Any chemical test would show that they haven't changed – so far as chemistry can tell. But to those who have put their trust in Jesus's promises, they have a new value, in much the same way as a piece of paper means something different to us when it has printed on it, 'I promise to pay the Bearer on demand the sum of One Pound.' In the Holy Communion service the bread is to us Christ's body, and the wine is to us his blood. Why? Because he promised!

The priest who presides at the Holy Communion is not a magician turning one thing into another. But as he repeats the story of the last supper, as he takes, and breaks, and pours, and gives, all the Christians present are caught up into the drama – for as we 'do this' here and now we are ourselves actors in the drama, not mere spectators. And into the midst of us, sinful and blind as we are, Jesus comes. The action of eating and drinking, in this wonderfully special setting, means a 'communion' or intimate fellowship with him. In much the same way, a handshake means: I want to be your friend. Or a salute means: I obey you. Or a kiss means: I love you. We gather as friends of one another and of Jesus. We obey his order, 'do this', as part of our whole attempt to live as he commanded.

Naturally we remember the last supper and the crucifixion of Jesus. We celebrate his perfect sacrifice made once for all upon the cross. But we can only *celebrate* his death – we can only call that Friday good – if we are convinced that he has been raised from the dead by the power and the glory of his Father and ours. Christians remember this particularly on Sunday, the first day of the week, which has replaced the Jewish Sabbath (Saturday), because on Sunday Christians first knew that they were reunited with Jesus after his crucifixion. Every Sunday is a little Easter. As we eat and drink in fellowship with our living Lord, and in the presence of our Father, we pray that we may be filled with the Holy Spirit – so that we, too, may love. As we feed on the divine life, now among us and in us, we who believe give thanks. And now we can say in the silence of our hearts: 'Here, Lord, is my body – for you. And here is my blood – for you.' That is the living sacrifice of ourselves.

An act so full of meaning has to be prepared for carefully. As Paul told the Corinthians: 'A man must test himself before eating his share of the bread and drinking from the cup.' We have come together to realise the presence of God, to whom (as the old prayer says) 'all hearts are open, all desires known'. So we pray together – as we ought already to have prayed in private – for the cleansing of our thoughts.

To help this, we are given the 'collect' or ancient prayer which 'collects' the thoughts of the Church for this particular day or week. We are given, too, a reading from 'the epistle' – an extract from one of the letters of St Paul or St John. It is read to us as it was originally read to a group of Christians. Then we stand to hear an extract from one of the gospels and to join in saying the creed which is the Church's response to this cleansing revelation of God in Jesus Christ.

After the creed we pray for the Church and for the world. We remember particularly all in authority, and all who suffer in body, mind or spirit. We pray for ourselves, for our families and friends, and for the dead, that in us all God's will may be done; and we rejoice at the faithful witness of the saints in every age, praying that we may share with them in God's eternal kingdom. There are no barriers around us as we gather for this Holy Communion. We are open to the world – and to heaven.

Then we confess what is wrong. Because we are sinners, we say before we come to this table: 'We are not worthy so much as to gather up the crumbs.' But the bread and the wine which have been made out of the wheat and the grapes can be used to express God's creating and forgiving love; and so we offer these symbols of our own life and work – for him to make clean and useful. In this trust, we dare to join the song which, in Luke's gospel (chapter 2), the shepherds hear in the field near Bethlehem: 'Glory to God in the highest. . . .' We join, too, in the song which, in the book of Isaiah (chapter 6), the prophet hears in the temple in Jerusalem: 'Holy, holy, holy. . . .' And as one climax in the service, we dare to join in the prayer which Jesus gave to his followers: 'Our Father. . . .'

Christians can turn to this feast in every conceivable variety of mood. People have taken part in the Holy Communion after being married, after being crowned, before a battle, and before dying. They have taken part in it while seated on the floor as a young people's group, while gathered around a kitchen table, while standing in a prison cell, while crowded together at a great open-air rally. Columbus did this while sailing to discover America, and we can do it before any sorrow or happiness, or before beginning a routine kind of week. And whatever our mood may be, we shall find that we have to adjust to the mood dictated by the Church's year – another source of variety in this endless, inexhaustible act.

In Advent when we wait for Christ's coming at Christmas, and in Lent when the days lengthen as we wait for Easter, the colour is solemn purple or blue, and we pray for the spirit of expectancy and discipline. At Christmas and Easter the colour in church is white; with great joy we recall him whose birth made us clean and whose death destroyed death's power to destroy us. At Whitsun, when the colour is red (for fire), we recall the gift of the Spirit, leading into all truth. On the Sundays after Trinity Sunday, when the colour is green (for life), we think of the practical consequences of our belief that God has revealed his glory in the undivided splendour of the Father, the Son and the Spirit.

Whatever our own mood may be, and whatever the Church's season may be, taking part in this feast is like medicine to the sick or light to the blind. It does not matter what we call this service – 'Holy Communion', or 'the Lord's Supper', or 'the Eucharist' (from the Greek for 'Thanksgiving'), or 'the Mass' (from the Latin for 'Sent'). This supreme act of Christian fellowship makes us more deeply thankful, and sends us out into the world in the power of the Holy Spirit. Those who have shared this feast find themselves called to live and work in such a way that God is praised and seen in his glory – when these

Christians are being the Body of Christ far away from any church building or service.

How often should we take part in the Holy Communion? Anglicanism leaves it to our own consciences. Some Christians who have prepared themselves carefully have found that they could not honestly do so very often – so they have not gone very often. But in Anglicanism today, more and more Christians are finding that it is best to go every Sunday to the Parish Communion. Then the Holy Communion becomes to them, all together, what it was for the first Christians and what it has been for so many millions: *the* Christian act. It is the Lord's own service on the Lord's own day.

14

We turn to the future

THE COMPLAINT is made that the Church clings to the past. If that is the whole truth about the Church, then it is a sentence of death. For to live, we must be active; to be active, we must have hope; and to have hope, we must turn to the future with zest. If the Church were to be a museum only, the stench of decay would probably be so depressing that fewer and fewer people would look into it. But that is *not* the whole truth!

The Christian Church has many solid reasons to be proud of its past. Jesus Christ told his followers to be like salt in the world, making history taste good, and to some extent that is what they have been. But great as the past is, the Church when it is true to its own message cannot cling to it. For the original message of the Church was about the future – about the coming of the kingdom of God, the beginning of God's complete rule. The first words spoken by Jesus in Mark's gospel (the first gospel written) are these: 'The time has come; the kingdom of God is upon you; repent and believe the Gospel.' That 'Gospel' or good news is about something bigger than the Church. The first Christians thought so highly of the Church to which they belonged that they pictured it as the bride of Christ – but with a passionate excitement they looked forward to something far better than the Church they knew. They looked forward to the total victory of Jesus. Almost the very last words of the Bible are these: ' "Come!" say the Spirit and the bride. "Come!" let each hearer reply. Amen. Come, Lord Jesus!'

It may be that mankind has a glorious future ahead on this planet – although it often looks as if man is about to commit suicide. Scientists believe that the earth will be able to support human life for another two thousand million years to come. And it may be that Christians yet to be born will bring a glory into the Church's tradition far greater than any yet seen; it may turn out that twentieth-century Christianity was extremely primitive. Whatever the future is to be on this earth, long or short, glorious or tragic, Christians believe that it will lead to only one destination. At the end will come the final proof that, in his essential claims about God and God's creation, and in what he said about the supreme importance and power of love, Jesus Christ was right. So all human history – all the Church, but also all mankind – will be judged by one standard: *how do you compare with Jesus Christ, who is man as God wants man to be?*

Writing to the Christians in Rome (chapter 8), Paul describes the Spirit given to Christians as 'the firstfruits of the harvest to come' – the bit of the crop that guarantees that the rest is on its way. In other words, the spiritual power which Christians do experience in their best moments is no more than a foretaste of what is promised. Paul writes of 'the splendour in store for us ... the liberty and splendour of the children of God'. He says that we are going to be Christ-like, so that Jesus may be 'the eldest among a large family of brothers'. He asks triumphantly: 'If God is on our side, who is against us? ... How can he fail to lavish upon us all he has to give? ... There is nothing in death or life ... in the world as it is or in the world as it shall be, in the forces of the universe, in heights or depths – nothing in all creation that can separate us from the love of God in Christ Jesus our Lord.'

According to the New Testament, the Church's own life is meant to be a foretaste of the future. The letter to the Ephesians includes in its first chapter this prayer: 'that you may know what is the hope to which God calls you, what the wealth and glory of the share he offers you among his people in their heritage, how vast the resources of his power open to us who trust in him ... so that he might display in the ages to come how vast are the resources of his grace, and how great is his kindness to us in Christ Jesus.' So a church building, set among people's homes, is meant to be a reminder of the future which is now open to all mankind. In particular, every Holy Communion is a meal for travellers – and a promise that God has prepared a banquet for all his children at the end.

In different periods people tend to want different things from the Church, because they hope for different things from the future. For example, when these islands and the rest of Europe were full of barbarians who killed and destroyed wherever they went, people longed for peace – and the peace of a monastery was a foretaste, a pledge, a guarantee of the peace of the world. When people's own homes showed how poor they were, and how close they lived to disease and death, they built and adorned churches. Many churches were palaces for God and his people. Their beauty was a foretaste, a pledge, a guarantee of the final 'City of God' – where no temple would be needed. It is interesting to think out what are the most powerful hopes of this generation. We still long for peace and plenty; indeed, war in our nuclear age and poverty on our rich planet seem to us outrageous. But now there is a special intensity of hope around the idea of *unity*.

We all know in our hearts that we desperately need a greater sense of community, so that all the different groups that make up modern society may work together for the common good, overcoming their prejudices and settling their disputes on the basis of fairness and justice. And we all know how completely the nations of the modern world depend on each other, despite their bitter suspicions and quarrels. We know that we need to share in order to survive. For this reason, the twentieth century has asked the Church: 'Do you have the secret of unity for a divided nation and a divided world? Are you yourselves united? Do you Christians love one another?'

Because the Church as we see it on this earth is *people*, not angels – ordinary people, not saints – the Church is always disappointing. The Church is so full of human imperfections that we can easily pick holes in it, complaining about what it does and about what it fails to do, condemning its failure. But we have to ask ourselves: if the fault lies with the people who make up the Church, are we ourselves any better? Are we in a position to criticise? Above all, are we entitled to stand aloof? Is it right for us to be proud that our hands are clean, when the reason is that we washed them too soon – or never did any work to get them dirty?

Each individual who is in touch with the Church is challenged for a few years to *be* the Church on this earth. The responsibility could not be greater, for according to the New Testament God has a purpose for everyone who is reached by the Church's message. It is not enough to criticise or applaud as spectators. The person who is challenged is expected to *do* something. God has a place for that one person – a place for him or her in the divine plan for the world, a place for him or her in the Church as described in Peter's first letter (chapter 2): 'a royal priesthood, a dedicated nation, and a people claimed by God for his own, to proclaim the triumphs of him who has called you out of darkness into his marvellous light.'

If that person turns away, as Judas Iscariot did, he or she turns to the darkness, at least for the time being. That person's place may be given to someone else, or that piece of work for God's rule on earth and for the Church may be left undone for ever. But if that person accepts the calling of God through the voice of Jesus – if that person hears his or her name, as the first followers of Jesus heard their Master say 'Simon Peter!' or 'Mary!' – that person turns to the light and to the future.

The Church is changing fast. It may seem like winter –

but actually it is spring. The new music that is sung in many churches nowadays is only a small example of the renewal that is going on. Another example of change is that more and more responsibility is being taken by lay members of the Church – the 'royal priesthood' of Peter's letter. It is no longer possible to 'leave it to the vicar'! In many ways lay members of the Church, particularly those who belong to the new generation, are using their imagination and courage. They are taking risks and making starts. Tact and perseverance are essential, for they have to persuade fellow-Christians who are conservative. But they are the people needed to rise to the future, to respond to the adventure of Jesus Christ.

Once when Jesus told a man to follow him, the man said that he would, one day – but he must stay at home until his father had died. Jesus replied that the future was more important. 'Follow me, and leave the dead to bury their dead.'

Of all the Christians who have lived so far, probably St Paul had the best reasons for taking pride in how he had followed Jesus. But this is what he wrote to the Philippians (3. 10–14), when he was near the end of his life, in prison in Rome. 'All I care for is to know Christ, to experience the power of his resurrection, and to share his sufferings. ... Forgetting what is behind me, and reaching out for what lies ahead, I press towards the goal to win the prize.' And that, surely, must be the spirit in which we are in the Church in our time. We get ready for the future, we reach out for what lies ahead – and, if need be, we forget the past.

But what should that mean in practice?

Since the Church is people, not buildings – people, not doctrines – what is supremely important is the *character* of Christians. Whether we are loving matters far more than anything else. How we think and behave as people among other people (who watch!) is more important than how often we go to church. What the world needs and wants is a Church of living stones – a Church made up of people full of love. This is also what Jesus wants from his friends, as John's gospel makes clear in chapter 15. 'This is my commandment: love one another, as I have loved you. There is no greater love than this, that a man should lay down his life for his friends. You are my friends, if you do what I command you.'

Since most of our lives when not sleeping or eating are spent working, the most important contribution we can make to the welfare and progress of the world is to do useful *work* – and do it honestly and thoroughly.

This is the case whether our work is in our home, in a factory, in an office, in a shop, in transport, or anywhere else. It is all serving other people, and so is serving the purposes of God. Very many Christians make their contribution through the professions which directly help others in their hours of need – as a priest, doctor, nurse, teacher or social worker. But thousands of other jobs are useful. Christian entertainers are needed, for example. So are Christian grocers, or miners, or politicians, or secretaries, or dustmen, or shop assistants, or businessmen, or waitresses, or pilots, or machine operators, or farmers, or postmen. ... Christians, when they offer themselves to God, do not offer only Sundays or the evenings – they offer their work. They offer themselves as hard workers, honest, thorough and skilful. That does not mean, however, that they never criticise anything to do with their work. On the contrary, Christians work with their eyes open. They may ask awkward questions. Are the wages paid fair wages? Are the relationships between the people involved in the work as friendly as possible? Are the products being made, or services being given, as good as they can be, for the benefit of the people who need them?

Sometimes it is impossible to escape being unemployed – God understands. And sometimes it is healthy and necessary to relax, with nothing to do – God knows that, too. But Jesus, as he bids farewell to his friends in John's gospel, speaks about what they will achieve by work, and it is right to extend the meaning of these words to cover all the work done faithfully by Christians. 'I am the vine, and you the branches. He who dwells in me, as I dwell in him, bears much fruit. . . . This is my Father's glory, that you may bear fruit in plenty. . . . I appointed you to go on and bear fruit, fruit that shall last.'

Since the world is a very practical place, Christians have to combine so that together they may set an example of *love at work*. A twentieth-century English saint, C. F. Andrews who was a famous missionary in India, used to say: 'love is the accurate estimate and supply of another's needs.' So Christians who work in the same place ought sometimes to get together, to ask themselves what their duty is in that place and how they can be better Christians at work. And Christians who live in the same district ought also to get together and ask themselves some practical questions. For a Christian congregation is meant to set an example to the neighbourhood in reaching and serving members of the community who need help.

When a congregation (or a group of congregations) organises a play group for pre-school children, or when it runs a Sunday School, or when it supports an adventure playground or expeditions for children in the school holidays, or when it arranges groups of young people (Cubs, Brownies, Scouts, Guides, the Church Lads' Brigade, the Boys' Brigade, a youth club, or any other group), or when it gathers a young wives' group or a women's fellowship or a branch of the Mothers' Union, or when it sponsors interesting activities for men (for example, through a branch of the Church of England Men's Society), or when it gets visitors to keep in regular touch with old people and to help them if asked – then something practical and something Christian is being done, and the Church is serving others according to the example of its Lord, who washed his own disciples' feet.

Just the same thing is happening whenever Christians struggle for better housing in the neighbourhood, or for justice between the nations of the world, or when they collect money for charities such as Christian Aid (the British Churches' own charity to give relief to the victims of disasters and to help the poor peoples of the world to develop their own countries). Christians can wash the world's feet by serving in local government or in voluntary help to the local social services or the local hospital, or by being active in the local branch of a political party or trade union. It is all needed today – and it is all work for a better tomorrow.

One problem faced by all the good causes in our country (some of which have just been mentioned) is the problem of how to recruit enough unpaid leaders and workers. Often such people volunteer from Christian congregations, and that is a good reason for being proud of the Church. Another problem faced by many fellowships is that their members are not regular and loyal enough; many members don't turn up at meetings and don't support activities. When Christians do take their responsibilities seriously, that is another good reason for being thankful that the Church can train us to be loyal.

Christians, if they are loyal to the Spirit in Christianity, follow their Lord modestly and happily. They do not consider themselves morally superior to others. They remember the words of Jesus in John's gospel: 'You did not choose me. I chose you.' They do not put on an air of gloom, or one of grim determination. They remember other words of Jesus: 'I have spoken to you, so that my joy may be in you, and your joy complete.' In a world full of rivalries, Christians have achieved much if they have set an example of humility. And in a world full of fears, Christians have achieved much if they have set an example of joy.

When we speak of the 'mission' of the Church, we mean what the Church is sent into the world to be and to do. It is sent into the whole world – to every nation, tribe, city, town or village without exception. Anglicans are reminded of their mission in six continents by the challenges of their own societies which send and support missionaries overseas. In Britain, the largest of these societies are the Church Missionary Society and the United Society for the Propagation of the Gospel (with the Society for Promoting Christian Knowledge specialising in Christian literature). The Church has a world-wide outreach. But equally, every congregation is challenged to undertake its own mission in its own neighbourhood, and every Christian has a mission to his or her own friends. This mission is an essential part of what it means to be the Church and to be a Christian. The task is urgent, and clear. It is to tell others about Jesus – chiefly by how we live and serve. We are not experts instructing completely ignorant people 'how to be good'; we are much more like a beggar who tells another beggar where there is food. We point by our lives to the source of our joy, and then the words come. They must come, because the message is so happy.

It is natural for a new generation to hope, and that is one of the reasons why the Church needs young people with their generosity, energy and daring. But Christian hope is not foolish optimism. That is why the Church also needs older people with their tested faithfulness. The world is a tough place, and in it anyone who wants to achieve anything worth achieving has to overcome many obstacles and has to possess patience. The courage of Christians is based not on expecting an easy life but on having a solid reason for going on being hopeful among the problems. In John's gospel (chapter 16), Jesus gives this reason when he tells his friends: 'You will be joyful, and no one shall rob you of your joy . . . I have told you all this so that in me you may find peace. In the world you will have trouble. But courage! The victory is mine; I have conquered the world.'

15

The heart of it all

THE SILENCE OF ETERNITY

You do look, my son, in a mov'd sort,
As if you were dismay'd: be cheerful, sir.
Our revels now are ended. These our actors,
As I foretold you, were all spirits and
Are melted into air, into thin air;
And, like the baseless fabric of this vision,
The cloud-capp'd towers, the gorgeous palaces,
The solemn temples, the great globe itself,
Yea, all which it inherit, shall dissolve
And, like this insubstantial pageant faded,
Leave not a rack behind. We are such stuff
As dreams are made on, and our little life
Is rounded with a sleep. . . .
        William Shakespeare (1564–1616)

OUT OF SILENCE A VOICE

Love bade me welcome; yet my soul drew back,
    Guilty of dust and sin.
But quick-ey'd Love, observing me grow slack
    From my first entrance in,
Drew nearer to me, sweetly questioning
    If I lack'd anything.

'A guest', I answered, 'worthy to be here':
  Love said, 'You shall be he'.
'I, the unkind, ungrateful? Ah, my dear,
  I cannot look on thee.'
Love took my hand, and smiling did reply,
  'Who made the eyes but I?'

'And know you not', says Love, 'Who bore the
    blame?'
  'My dear, then I will serve.'
'You must sit down', says Love, 'and taste my meat.'
  So I did sit and eat.

George Herbert (1593–1633)

MAN SPEAKS TO GOD

Wilt thou forgive that sin where I begun,
Which was my sin, though it were done before?
Wilt thou forgive that sin, through which I run,
And do run still: though still I do deplore?
When thou hast done, thou hast not done,
    For I have more.

Wilt thou forgive that sin which I have won
Others to sin? and made my sin their door?
Wilt thou forgive that sin which I did shun
A year, or two: but wallowed in, a score?
When thou hast done, thou hast not done,
    For I have more.

I have a sin of fear, that when I have spun
My last thread, I shall perish on the shore;

But swear by thyself, that at my death thy Son
Shall shine as He shines now, and heretofore;
And, having done that, thou hast done,
    I fear no more.
           John Donne (1571?–1631)

MAN TRUSTS GOD

Strong Son of Good, immortal Love,
  Whom we, that have not seen thy face,
  By faith, and faith alone, embrace,
Believing where we cannot prove;

Thine are these orbs of light and shade;
  Thou madest life in man and brute;
  Thou madest Death; and lo, thy foot
Is on the skull that thou hast made.

Thou wilt not leave us in the dust:
  Thou madest man, he knows not why;
  He thinks he was not made to die;
And thou hast made him: thou art just.

Thou seemest human and divine,
  The highest, holiest manhood thou;
  Our wills are ours, we know not how;
Our wills are ours, to make them thine.

Our little systems have their day;
  They have their day, and cease to be:
  They are but broken lights of thee,
And thou, O Lord, art more than they.

We have but faith; we cannot know;
   For knowledge is of things we see;
   And yet we trust it comes from Thee,
A beam in darkness: let it grow.

Let knowledge grow from more to more,
   But more of reverence in us dwell;
   That mind and soul, according well,
May make one music as before,

But vaster. We are fools and slight;
   We mock thee when we do not fear:
   But help thy foolish ones to bear,
Help thy vain worlds to bear thy light.
                Alfred Tennyson (*1809–92*)

OUR CHOICE

Space is the Whom our loves are needed by,
   Time is our choice of How to love and Why.
                W. H. Auden (*1907–73*)

Index